A SURGEON'S
WAKE UP CALL

Thomas Calhoun, MD, MS, FACN, FACS

authorHOUSE®

AuthorHouse™
1663 Liberty Drive
Bloomington, IN 47403
www.authorhouse.com
Phone: 833-262-8899

Published by AuthorHouse 04/18/2022

ISBN: 978-1-6655-5750-4 (sc)
ISBN: 978-1-6655-5748-1 (hc)
ISBN: 978-1-6655-5749-8 (e)

Library of Congress Control Number: 2022907521

Print information available on the last page.

To Wil "Jenk" Jenkins, my best friend, who died from metastatic prostate cancer on July 7, 2020, at age eighty-eight, and to my tennis buddies and medical colleagues and their families who also died from prostate cancer.

INTRODUCTION

"Dr. Calhoun, can you hold for Dr. Fangonil, please?", the voice on the other end of the phone asked. I sometimes answered the phone myself as there were occasions when the office manager and receptionist were tied up with other patients (or more likely with insurance offices trying to get authorization for consultation or surgical procedure), but I had no problem holding.

Alex, Dr. Alexander Fangonil, who has graciously given me permission to use his name and his experiences in writing this book—and I had been practicing in our respective fields of surgery for over twenty years, he in urology and I in general surgery.

It was interesting I thought in that short time I was holding—less than fifteen seconds—how with flashbacks one can recall so much information.

The phone had rung at about 3:00 a.m. The caller said, "Doctor Calhoun, this is Annie Fangonil. Alex has an incarcerated inguinal hernia. It happened during our flight from the Philippines last night. We're on the way to the emergency room at Providence Hospital."

Annie, Alex's wife, had worked in the office with Dr. Fangonil since he started practice twenty years earlier, so she was quite familiar with medical terminology, and I am sure Alex told her what was happening. I told her I would meet them at the emergency room, a fifteen-minute drive from our house.

Providence Hospital is one of two Catholic hospitals in Washington, DC, having received its original charter from President Lincoln in 1861. (Georgetown University is the other.) Providence closed in August 2018 and began offering urgent outpatient care services later that year.

I arrived at the emergency room around 3:30 a.m., spoke with Annie briefly, and proceeded to evaluate Alex. Indeed, he had an incarcerated right inguinal hernia incorporating the right testicle. He told me the hernia had been present for some years but asymptomatic—that is, causing no pain or discomfort—and he had decided not to have it repaired surgically.

Hernia is a condition in which part of an organ is displaced and protrudes through a weak spot in the surrounding muscles or connective tissue. We discussed the planned surgery, and he initiated the thought that the right testicle might have to be removed. The operative permit stated that a repair of the right inguinal hernia and possible right orchiectomy would be performed.

By 5:00 a.m., we had moved to the operating room, where following appropriate general anesthesia, the hernia was repaired.

Assisting me was Dr. Tomas Thomasian, who had been a surgeon for the shah of Iran before that regime ended and was at that point working as a surgical assistant at Providence Hospital here in northeast Washington, DC.

Dr. Thomasian expired in 2019.

Alex and I were residents in our respective fields at Freedmen Hospital at Howard University in DC from 1964 through 1968. Before the surgery, he told me he remembered an article I had published some years earlier about megaherniae ("Meg").[1] Alex has been my urologist for the past twenty years, and I have annually made the visit to his office for that dreaded digital rectal exam (DRE) to evaluate the status of my prostate gland. There was also a referral to my primary physician for the annual bloodletting to include the prostate specific antigen (PSA). My last PSA was 4.0 (0.0–4.0 normal range ng/mL), but over the past year, it had increased to 8.0. I will say more about the PSA later, in the prostate section.

Several years earlier, I had developed enlargement of the gland consistent with benign prostatic hypertrophy (BPH).

---

[1] Calhoun, T. et al., "The Use of Pneumoperitoneum in the Treatment of Megaherniae," *JNMA* (January 1975) 66:16–18.

I had been taking Hytrin (terazosin)[2] for several years but had changed to Flomax (tamsulosin), both alpha-1 blockers specifically for BPH that basically help relax the muscles in the prostate and bladder and make it easier to "pee."

For the academically oriented, alpha blockers keep the hormone norepinephrine or noradrenaline from tightening the muscles in the walls of the smaller arteries and veins.[3] From my review of the literature, the only beta blocker used for treatment of BPH is Carvedilol, primarily used for treating heart failure.[4] Beta blockers target epinephrine or adrenaline.

After the DRE, during which Alex felt some irregularities in the prostate that had not been present in the past, and due to the increase in the PSA from 4 to 8 in one year, we decided on a biopsy of the gland.

As I waited for Alex to pick up the phone, I wondered what the call was about because I did not know the results of the biopsy.

"Tommm ..." There was always a prolonged enunciation of my first same, which was Alex's way of a friendly greeting. "Alex here. How are you?"

After pleasantries and inquiries into how our families were doing, he asked if Shirley, my wife, and I could come in to see him. I knew from that request and his wanting to see both of

---

2 https://www.webmd.com>drugs>flomax-oral>details.

3 https://www.mayoclinic.org.side-effects>drg_20066415.

4 Frishman, W. H., *NEJM*, 1998; 399: 1759–65.

us that the biopsy was likely positive for cancer. As a physician who had been practicing for over thirty years at the time, I had often made a similar call to my patients.

A few days later, Shirley and I met with him and discussed the findings. The pathology report of the biopsy was prostate cancer, Gleason's Score 5, a low-grade carcinoma; clinically, Stage 1. (Staging and Gleason's Score, various diagnostic measures and treatment options, will be further discussed in the section on the prostate.)

We discussed the various options for treating prostate cancer and decided to have external beam radiation therapy (EBRT), which for me would be forty-three days. We elected to start after the Christmas holidays, in February 2005 at the Washington Hospital Center, waiting several months after the prostate biopsy to allow for adequate healing.

The following in diary form is the chronology of my experiences during my forty-three days of EBRT.

CHAPTER 1

I had stopped practicing surgery and was working as a full-time medical director in the District of Columbia Department of Health (DCDOH) with an emphasis on emergency preparedness. I was hired for the position in February 2003 following discussions with Dr. Michael Richardson, then the director of DCDOH, based primarily on my having had training in the US Army in chemical, biological, radiological, and nuclear warfare. (Dr. Richardson moved from DC in 2003, and I have no knowledge of his present location.)

In September 2001, the nation experienced 9/11 followed by the anthrax event in DC in October 2001, when two African American males died from inhalation of anthrax spores. (See newspaper article.) Furthermore, the United States was conducting a full-scale war against the nation of Iraq and Saddam Hussein, who was suspected of preparing to use the biological agent smallpox, for which there is no cure, against his adversaries.

Smallpox is a severe febrile illness (38.5–40.5°C) with flulike symptoms and a rash starting in the mucosa of the mouth, face, and hands caused by the variola virus. It was eradicated worldwide in the late 1970s through vaccinations with the live vaccinia vaccine virus. The vaccinia virus does not cause smallpox.

One of the first things I did after being hired was to get vaccinated with the vaccinia virus against smallpox. Other than a bit of soreness at the injection site and a low-grade fever the next day, I had no side effects of the vaccination.

During the three weeks following vaccination, Shirley visited her parents in Las Vegas, Nevada. We decided on that before I was vaccinated because vaccinia is a live virus, and whereas it cannot cause smallpox, it can cause severe complications if the site is not properly cared for, and for other individuals who may be exposed. It takes from seventeen to twenty-one days for the scab to detach from the site revealing the scar, at which time it is safe to mingle with others.[5]

When I was medical director for the Emergency Health and Medical Services Administration (EHMSA), we vaccinated about a hundred individuals from the State Department here in DC, and other civilians who were preparing to go to Iraq.

---

[5] www.bt.cdc.gov/training/smallpoxvaccine/reactions. See M. J. Roy, *Physician's Guide to Terrorist Attack* (Totowa, NJ: Humana Press, 2004), 198–220.

CHAPTER 2

◆

Start of 43 Days of External Beam Radiation Therapy (ERBT)

Day 1
Monday, February 28, 2005

Awake at 5:45 a.m. After stretching said my morning prayers while still in bed. For April, the weather was still a bit chilly, so I put on my tan corduroy trousers,[6] a vest over my white turtleneck sweater, my black-and-tan scarf, and my brown leather flight jacket, and I left for Mass.

I arrived at the Basilica of the Shrine of the Immaculate Virgin Mary on Harewood Road and Michigan Avenue Northeast (NE), in time for the 7:00 a.m. mass.

---

[6] French *cord du roi*, "cord for kings," from cord and *duroy*, a coarse woolen cloth made in England in the eighteenth century). https://kingspinsshow.com>historyof-corduroy. https://en.wikipedia.org>wiki>corduroy.

Mass was over at about 7:31 a.m., and I went to our Lady of Lourdes Chapel just to the right when exiting the Crypt Church, a replica of the site of the appearances of the Virgin Mary to Saint Bernadette Soubirous in Lourdes, France,[7] from February 11 through July 15, 1858.

I prayed the first three decades of the Joyful Mysteries of the rosary and then left for the Washington Hospital Center (WHC) to begin the forty-three days of external beam radiation therapy (EBRT) I had elected to have.

Several days earlier, I had gone to WHC and completed the requisite paperwork, insurance information, etc., and was given my individual computer card. I was able to park in the section marked Cancer Patients Only near the entrance, and I proceeded to the radiation therapy area.

After signing in, I went to the men's dressing area and slipped into one of those demeaning hospital gowns that open in the back though I was able to keep my shorts on. There, I met three young women, Tina, Monica, and Carrie, who gave me instructions. I left my clothes in a locker and walked into the treatment room in my socks, but I was told that henceforth, I could keep my shoes on and take them off once I reached the treatment area.

My treatment time was for 8:20 a.m. Lying prone on the X-ray table, I was told I would get an initial series of X-rays covering the sites on which I had I had initially been given

---

[7] https://en.wikipedia.org>Our_Lady_of_Lourdes.

tattoos and transparent tape strips at the anterior superior spine, the apex of the bladder, and both hips just below the trochanters. I would then proceed to receive seven series of radiation approximately forty seconds each at the seven sites around the prostate as marked with the tattoos and tape.

I was given a blue concentration ring, a wooden ring about seven inches in diameter, as a means to help me keep both hands still over my chest. I kept my rosary in my hands and would start a mystery of the rosary[8] as soon as treatment began. Both legs would be placed in an air mattress–type restraint helping me keep still. A rolled towel was placed under my neck ... No pillow was provided. (See images.)

I was told total radiation time would be five to seven minutes.

On the ceiling was an image of a serene, blue sky with a few white clouds.

The X-ray table did not rotate but did move up and down.

The radiation machine, the 21 EX Linear Accelerator, moved in multiple directions to provide beams of ionizing radiation to the seven sites.

---

[8] *Catholic Encyclopedia Dictionary.* The rosary is a series of prayers in honor of the Blessed Virgin Mary containing fifteen decades each consisting of one Our Father, ten Hail Marys, and one Glory Be to the Father, referred to as Mysteries. There are four Mysteries—the Glorious, Joyful, Luminous, and Sorrowful each commemorating a significant event in the birth, life, passion, and death and resurrection of Jesus Christ. The Glorious Mystery is also dedicated to the Holy Spirit and the Blessed Virgin Mary.

I was able to complete three decades of the Joyful Mysteries of the rosary at the completion of the seven minutes of therapy.

After completion of this first treatment cycle and getting dressed, I had my parking ticket stamped and received directions to the second-floor lab, for blood to be drawn for a complete blood count. I was told this would occur frequently. Also, I was given an instruction manual and notepaper for a daily diary if desired, but I told the young woman at the desk that I had previously been given the manual and notepaper when I had a simulation of what was to come.

I proceeded to the office at DOH for work feeling nothing unusual.

It was still snowing but not enough to impair traffic.

Office work that day was mainly reading emails and finalizing a presentation on risk management and incident reporting to the staff.

I left the office at 4:30 p.m. and stopped by the National Shrine for the 5:10 mass. I joined a group praying of the rosary, which was ongoing. Mass ended about 6:00 pm, and I arrived home at about 6:15 joining Shirley, who was watching the news.

We ate fried chicken, red beans and rice, and biscuits with jelly, all left over from Popeye's the previous day. Dessert was butter pecan ice cream.

Shirley and I talked about how our day went, and she went up to bed around 8:50. I watched *24*, a hit TV show that did not interest Shirley. The show was a sci-fi thriller with the main character, Jack Bauer, hunting down international terrorists. Domestic terrorism was not being addressed in a major way, the Oklahoma bombing incident notwithstanding.[9] This was before 9/11.

After watching a bit of the ten o'clock news, I showered and went up to bed with Shirley. I read a few chapters of *Fatima, in Lucia's Own Words*,[10] and I prayed a few prayers to St. Joseph and Mother Lange.

I fell asleep around 11:00 p.m.

Day 2
Tuesday, March 1, 2005

I started the day at 5:30 a.m. with stretching and morning prayers while still in bed. I said seven Glory Be's and seven prayers to my guardian angel, whom I call G2. I don't have any reason for the name.

After shaving and showering, I left for the 7:00 a.m. mass at the National Shrine. It was very cold with lots of snow on the ground.

---

[9] Oklahoma City bombing: Facts, Motive, Timothy McVeigh https://www.britannica.com>event>Oklahoma-City-5.

[10] *Fatima, in Lucia's Own Words*, Fr. Louis Kondor, SVD, ed., Postulation Centre, Fatima, Portugal, April 1963.

After Mass, I said three decades of the Sorrowful Mysteries of the rosary in route to WHC for day two of my treatment. I thought it interesting that of all the times I had gone to WHC for meetings or to see Shirley when she was hospitalized there for pneumonia, I always drove by the parking spaces marked Cancer Patients Only. I'd never had a thought of having to park in one of those spaces as a cancer patient myself.

I didn't feel sick, and thankfully, I have not focused on having cancer. As a general surgeon, I am fully aware of cancer in its many forms, and I have helped operate on many patients with prostate cancer, involving the rectum, many with post-irradiation proctitis, sometimes having to fashion a colostomy, a surgical procedure where an opening, a stoma, of the large bowel is made and brought out through the abdominal wall usually in the left lower quadrant, and the distal part of the bowel is closed.[11] If the patient recovers from the event requiring the colostomy, the bowel can be reconstituted; however, in some instances, it may be permanent.

Any surgery in an area of post-radiation therapy should be avoided whenever possible as healing often does not go well.

My treatment started at 8:20 a.m. in the Alpha Room with Tina, Krista, and Ralph; I met the latter two for the first time then.

---

[11] www.healthline.com>health>colostomy. www.htpps://en.wikipedia.org/wiki/colostomy.

The position was again prone, my gown up to the umbilicus and shorts down to midthigh. Again, with my rosary in hand, I was given the blue circular hand support and cautioned to keep still and breathe normally. I guess it is reflex to want to assist in moving oneself to get in the proper position, but I was told gently but firmly, "Don't help us. We will move you," which they did using the draw sheet on which I was lying.

Two clean towels were put in place, one on my abdomen covered by my gown, the other midthigh leaving exposed the tattooed and taped areas as I previously noted.

As the linear accelerator began its trekking, first for the scout film and then for the seven forty-second treatment cycles, I was praying the Sorrowful Mysteries of the rosary.[12], [13]

Everything was done in seven or eight minutes, and I dressed, had my parking ticket stamped, and left for work. I stopped at the deli for the *Washington Post*, two donuts, scrambled eggs and potatoes, and decaf coffee.

---

[12] Robert Feeny, "Saint Dominic and the Rosary," Catholic.Net/rcc/periodicals. Faith/0910-96, article 11html. www.https://en.Wikipedia.org.History-of-the-Rosary. According to the Catholic Dominican tradition, in 1208, the rosary was given to St. Dominic in an apparition, a supernatural or ghostlike appearance, by the Blessed Virgin Mary.

[13] simplycatholic.com/the-rosary-and the-battle-of-Lepanto. A widely accepted miracle involving the rosary occurred on October 7, 1751. The Venetian Catholic navy, made up of an alliance of fleets from Spain and Italy, defeated a much larger Muslim fleet from Turkey after Pope Pius V asked the Christian faithful to pray the rosary. The victory is celebrated as a feast day in Catholic history, and October 7 is designated as the feast of Our Lady of the Rosary. simplycatholic.com/the-rosary-and the-battle-of-Lepanto.

After breakfast and scanning the *Post*, I caught up on my emails. At 11:40, I walked the ten minutes it took to get to St. Aloysius Gonzaga Catholic Church for the noon mass.[14]

I feel wonderfully blessed that on many occasions I have been able to get to Mass and Communion twice a day and benefit from the exercise of this brisk walk. A prayer I often pray during this walk is one reportedly given to St. Gertrude the Great by Jesus: "O Eternal Father, I offer Thee the most precious blood of Your Son Jesus, along with all the masses said today for all the Souls in Purgatory, for sinners through-out the land, for sinners in the Universal Church and for those in my home and my family."[15] Our Lord said this prayer would free 1,000 souls from purgatory[16] each time it was prayed, and 200 sinners would be given the grace to repent and I try to pray it often.

---

[14] http://en.wikipedia.org/wiki/Aloysius_Gonzaga. St. Aloysius Gonzaga was born on March 9, 1569, ordained as a Jesuit priest on November 25, 1585, and died on June 21, 1591. He was canonized and declared the patron of Christian youth by Pope Benedict XIII. His feast day is June 21, which happens to be the birthday of my wife, Shirley.

[15] St. Gertrude was a Benedictine nun and mystic born January 6, 1256, and died around November 17, 1302. She is reported to have been canonized in 1677 by Pope Clement XII. http://en.wikipedia.org/wiki/Gertrude_theGreat#cite_note-prayer-18. Pope Benedict XIV gave her the name Gertrude the Great to distinguish her from the abbess of Hackeborn and because of the depth of her spiritual and theological insight.

[16] Roman Catholics believe purgatory is a state or place where individuals who died in God's friendship are assured of salvation but who still have need of purification before entering heaven. https://wikipedia.org>wiki>purgatory.

I spent the rest of the day reviewing the policies of the department.

I received an email from Dan, the interim chief medical officer for the DC Department of Health wishing me well as I began my treatment.

I got home around 6:00 pm and watched the news with Shirley; we chatted about the day's activities. After showering and reading from *Fatima, in Lucia's Own Words*, I turned in about 10:30.

Day 3 Wednesday, March 2, 2005
Wednesday March 2, 2005

I started the day at 5:30 a.m. with stretching and morning prayers while still in bed. I said seven Glory Be's and seven prayers to my guardian angel.

After shaving and showering, I was out the door at 6:45 and en route to Mass at the National Shrine. As usual, I placed some bread crumbs around the tree to the right of the front steps. Because of the snow, I cleared an area on the walkway for the crumbs.

I arrived at the shrine for the 7:00 a.m. mass and afterward prayed three decades of the Glorious Mystery. I planned to finish the third and fourth at the WHC.

Outside the Crypt Chapel, where Mass is held, is the shrine is a statue of St. Katharine Drexel, whose feast day is March

2. She was born on November 26, 1852, in Philadelphia to a family that owned a banking fortune. Her uncle, Anthony Joseph Drexel, founded Drexel University.[17] She became a novice with the Catholic Sisters of Mercy and ultimately, the Sisters of the Blessed Sacrament, dedicated to the welfare of American Indians and African Americans.

Inside, I kept my shoes on until I checked in at the treatment area, that day with the Alpha Team Group. I was told this was the group in which I would complete my forty-three days of treatment. The pretreatment routine was the same.

I asked how forty-three days of treatment had been established and learned it was arrived at via various clinical trials with multiple individuals who had similar stages and Gleason scores for prostate cancer as I had and PSAs in the range I had, 8, increasing in the past two years from 4.0 ng/mL. I also was told that I would receive a total of 180 RADS, or approximately 4.186 RADs per day.[18]

---

[17] http://en.wikipedia.org.wiki/Katherine_Drexel. "She financed more than 60 missions and schools around the United States as well as founding Xavier University of Louisiana, in New Orleans, the only historically Black Catholic University in the United States." She is known as the patron saint of racial justice and philanthropists. https://www.britannica.com> ... Sociology & Society. She died on March 3, 1955, and was canonized by Pope John Paul II, now St. Pope John Paul II, on October 1, 2000, the second American-born saint. St. Elizabeth Ann Seaton was the first, born in New York City in 1774 and canonized in 1975.

[18] A RAD is a unit of absorbed dose of ionizing radiation equal to an energy of 100 ergs per gram of irradiated material. www.en.wikipedia.org>wiki. Rad (unit).

After completing the day's course, I spoke with Dr. Michael P, the White radiation therapist, who indicated he had graduated from Meharry Medical College, my alma mater, in 1985, which was a comforting and interesting anecdote. I had graduated in 1963, so we spent some time talking about changes at Meharry since 1963.

When I was in medical school, there were no White medical students at Meharry and only six Black females in our class. We did have an occasional White physician from Vanderbilt University Medical School who gave us lectures, one I remember in urology.[19]

I arrived at the office about 8:50 a.m. after stopping at the cafeteria for scrambled eggs, potatoes, sausage links, a donut, decaf coffee, and the *Washington Post*.

At about 11:30, I received a call from Sharon from my old office at the EHMSA at 64 New York Avenue across the street from my current office at the Addiction Prevention and Rehabilitation Administration (APRA). She told me there had been another mercury spill at the Cardoza High School in NW DC.

The first incident was in October 2003.

I was tasked by the director of the Department of Health (DOH) to report to the site as the incident commander.

---

[19] The word *urology* is from the Greek *ouron*, urine and *aoyia-logia*, the study of. Urology is the branch of medicine and physiology concerned with the function and disorders of the urinary system. www.en.wikipedia.org/wiki/urology.

The incident commander directs the incident command system,[20] a standardized approach to the command, control, and coordination of emergency responses. This is a modular system and can be used in any declaration of an emergency or disaster.

In route to the site, I was told by staff via phone that the DOH director was home sick with what appeared to be the flu.

Mercury, also called quicksilver, is a chemical element identified as Hg, derived from the Latin name *hydrargyrum* or liquid silver.[21] It combines with silver to from an amalgam, or liquid alloy, which has been used in dentistry. It has various industrial uses. The most common cause of mercury poisoning is from ingesting too much methylmercury from various seafoods. Exposure may also occur from broken thermometers, absorption through the skin, or inhaling mercury vapors. Neurological effects are frequently noted.

Normal blood levels for mercury are less than 10 nanograms per milliliter though dentists and those who work around mercury may show values up to 15 without symptoms. If mercury is noted in hair samples or urine along with elevated blood values, immediate and thorough investigation must be instituted. There is no cure for mercury poisoning, but

---

[20] https://en.wikipedia.org>iki>Incident-Command_System.
[21] www.healthline.com>health>mercury-poisoning.

chelation therapy is helpful wherein there is binding of the toxic agent with a chelation solution.[22]

In October 2003, Ballou High School in SE DC was closed for three weeks due to exposure to mercury vapors; about forty individuals had been screened with blood and urine levels. Fortunately, no one required any medical management from the exposure.

Following investigation, it was determined that a student had "obtained, without permission, about 250 milli-Liters of Mercury from the Chemistry Lab" on a Friday afternoon and had visited some friends exposing them to the mercury. Multiple households had to be evacuated, one of which had a cat, which required much time and energy to catch. Those evacuated were housed in a hotel in DC for about three weeks before it was deemed safe for them to return to their homes.

I was Medical Director of the EHMSA at the time, so I was quite prepared for the Cardoza event. (See image.) I provided information to the local media and press at noon, 6:30 p.m., and 10:30 p.m., when my day there ended.

During this time, approximately seven hundred students and staff were screened for mercury vapor inhalation by means of hand-held Lumex machines by members of the DC DOH and fire/hazard teams from the fire department.[23]

---

[22] www.webmd.com>guide>what-is-chelation-therapy.

[23] www.michigan.gov>documents>mich.

The Lumex machine measures vapor concentrations of mercury and reports these values as nanograms per cubic meter and as micrograms per cubic meter. Eighty-eight people were found to have readings on their clothes or shoes of one microgram per cubic meter of mercury vapor and would have been evaluated by DOH medical and nursing staff. Two were young females who were pregnant and were advised to make an immediate appointment with their primary care physicians (PCP) or obstetricians. Others who noted any problems were advised to follow up with their PCPs. No medical problems were identified that warranted any onsite medical care or hospital transport.

For my efforts, when I left that night, I found $30 parking ticket under my windshield wiper even though I had my Police Parking tag exposed ... Thanks a lot!

After arriving home and showering, I had supper and a brief conversation with Shirley, who was almost asleep. I read from the Acts of the Apostles,[24] the events of Stephen's stoning, and a few pages from *Fatima, in Lucia's Own Words.*

---

[24] Acts 8:56–59.

Day 4
March 3, 2005 Thursday

I started my day at 5:40 with stretching and morning exercises as usual—about seven minutes of stretching in bed, arms, legs, flexing and extending the knees, rotating the hips, exercises a physical therapist at Providence taught me in 2003 after I hurt my back playing tennis. These were recommended after I had a laminectomy with a discectomy of L5, S1, on June 20, 1990, back surgery performed by Dr. Gary D, chief of neurosurgery at Freedmen's Hospital, Howard University, in DC. The surgery was successful; it relieved pressure on the fourth and fifth lumbar and first and second sacral nerves in the lower back. I had not had any further back issues and was playing tennis again in three months. My concerns were about any potential effect the radiation would have on my playing.

After 7:00 a.m. mass at the shrine, I prayed four decades of the rosary, and by the time I arrived at WHC to begin therapy, I had completed the fifth decade.[25]

Thursday is the week day masses are offered for priests, for their spiritual, emotional, and physical health and for more vocations to the priesthood and religious orders.

---

[25] https://washington.org>dc-guide-to-basicila-national-. https://www.gcatholic. org>churches>bas. The Basilica of the National Shrine to the Immaculate Conception is one of the ten largest Roman Catholic churches in North America located in DC. There are eighty chapels in the basilica.

The usual seven rotations of therapy began at 8:00 am. I was called early having arrived and checked in at 7:45.

After therapy, I stopped at the 64 New York NE Deli for a carry-out breakfast, the usual as previously noted.

I wore a coat and tie as I had a feeling there would be more media interaction related to the mercury spill. I was right. At 9:45, I was called by Leila, DOH's public information officer (PIO), to come to her office for live interviews with Channel 5 and Channel 7 TV stations.

A *hot wash*—brief discussions of key issues related to the event by DOH personnel—was scheduled for 10:00 a.m. I chaired that group but had to leave at 10:20 as Leila called again stating that we would have to go to the studio of Channel 7. It turned out that we did not have to go to Channel 5 as they were in the lobby of DOH's office building. We responded to questions related to the mercury spill for about ten minutes.

Since the daily events were ongoing, I had been given the green light by the PIO to answer the questions, always being transparent and honest with my responses. If I did not know the correct answer or did not have the information, I said I would get back with them with the information.

I never speculated.

There were no individuals from Channel 7, so after the interview with Channel 5, I went back to my office at APRA.

The remainder of the day was essentially uneventful as was the evening at home, so I turned in around 10:30 p.m.

Day 5
Friday, March 4, 2005

The morning began as usual, with stretching, other exercises as I have previously noted, then a shave and shower, and I was out the door about 6:30 for the 7:00 mass at the shrine. My attire was coat and tie as I was anticipating more media and press coverage of the mercury spill.

Since it was Friday, I prayed the first three Sorrowful Mysteries of the rosary today in Our Lady of Sorrows Chapel[26] in the Upper Church before leaving for therapy, finishing the fourth and fifth mysteries by the time I arrived at WHC; and luckily, finding a space in the Cancer Patients Only parking area.

I completed the fifth day of therapy and noted that thus far, I had not had any unusual symptoms.

There would be two more news conferences that day but no further information about any individuals exposed to the mercury spill was forthcoming from the fire/hazard unit, so I was able to get to the 5:15 mass at the shrine and then home for a quiet Friday evening with Shirley.

My next therapy was to be on Monday the 7th, but I expected some interaction with the media on the weekend for an update on the Mercury spill.

---

[26] https://en.wikipedia.org>wiki>Our__Lady_of_Sorrows.

Saturday, March 6, 2005

There was no therapy that day, but there was a media and press conference for updates on the mercury spill at noon.

Physically and emotionally, I felt well, feeling no ill effects from radiation therapy thus far.

Sunday, March 7, 2005

Up at about 6:15, stretching and prayed the Glorious Mysteries of the rosary, then showered, shaved and got dressed … Shirley was awake about 8:15.

Today, we would be attending the 10:30 a.m. Rose Mass and Awards Brunch at the Church of the Little Flower, St. Therese of Lisieux,[27] in Bethesda, Maryland, about a twenty-minute drive from home.

At this Mass, health care providers, members of the Catholic John Carroll Society, are formally recognized "for outstanding service to the Washington Archdiocesan Health Care Network."

---

[27] https://en.wikipedia.org>wiki>Therese of Lisieux. The biblical meaning of Theresa is "Gift of God." She was born on January 2, 1873, and died on September 30, 1897, at age twenty-four. She considered herself as a "little flower of Jesus," and when she entered the Carmelite Monastery, she chose the name "Therese of the child Jesus and the Holy Face." She was canonized by Pope Pius XI on May 17, 1925, and designated the youngest person to be proclaimed a doctor in the Catholic Church. https://Britannica.com> … Religious_Beliefs.

As one of the original members of the beginning of the network, I was recognized with an awards plaque on March 21, 2001. (See copy of plaque.)

It was the first time the event was not held at St. Patrick's Church[28] in downtown DC, where Monsignor Peter Vaghi, chaplain of the John Carroll Society, was the pastor. (He is now the pastor of the Church of the Little Flower in Bethesda, Maryland.) The day was sunny with beautiful blue skies and temperatures in the low forties, and a good turnout.

After Mass and the post-ceremonial conversations, it was around 1:45 p.m. by the time I got the car and picked up Shirley.

After we arrived home, I changed from the gray pinstriped suit and read the Sunday paper. Later, I went to the National Shrine to attend the 4:30 mass, and then to a drug store to get some personal supplies.

As I was leaving Mass, I received a phone call from Leila, the PIO, that more mercury had been detected at Cardoza Senior High School in NW DC.

On Saturday, based on levels of mercury detected by the Environmental Protective Agency (EPA), which ranged from 1–4 micrograms per cubic meter late Friday, all were now

---

[28] St. Patrick, "Apostle of Ireland." https://en.wikipedia.org>wiki>Saint_Patrick. https://www.britannica.com>Saints&Popes. St. Patrick's feast day, March 17, is a celebration of Irish culture with parades and drinking. He was never canonized by the Catholic Church because in the era in which he lived, there was no formal canonization process in the Catholic Church.

recordings below 1 microgram per cubic meter with an average of 0.005 micrograms per cubic meter. The levels recorded that Sunday afternoon in a classroom and the basement of 2–4 micrograms per cubic meter indicated that the school was not safe to reopen, and this information was relayed to the media.

There was a criminal investigation underway to determine who was responsible for the spill and how such an event could have occurred to prevent it's happening again.

The remainder of Sunday evening was uneventful.

Day 6
Monday March 7, 2005

Up at 5:45 for stretching and morning prayers. Today is the feast day of Saints Perpetua and Felicity.[29] After shaving and showering, I left home at about 6:30 and fed the birds. I noted some flowers blossoming, a sign of an early spring. I arrived at the shrine in time for the 7:00 mass.

I prayed four decades of the rosary in the chapel dedicated to Our Mother of Africa, thinking about the strife and suffering in Darfur, in the western part of Sudan (Arabic, "Land of the Fur … Land of the Blacks").[30]

---

[29] en.wikipedia.org/wiki/Perpetua_and_Felicity.

[30] https://www.britannica.com> Historical Places. The bronze statue of Our Mother of Africa holding the child Jesus was donated to the National Shrine in 1997 by African American Catholics. Fashioned by Edward Dwight, one of the sculptors, it shows the experiences of African Americans from the time of slavery to the civil rights

After I checked in at the treatment site at about 7:45, a number of the staff commented on having seen me on TV over the weekend with the news conferences about the mercury incident at the high school.

I had my treatment in the Beta Room as the Alpha machine needed servicing. Treatment is the same as previously noted; environmentally however, the overhead ceiling had a wider and more serene blue-sky appearance.

I had a brief discussion with Dr. P. I told him that I had been seeing softer stools since a few days previously, and he indicated that that was about what was expected. I also had blood drawn on the second floor for testing by a tech from Grenada.

After arriving at the office, I ate a breakfast of a link of sausage, eggs, potatoes, fruit, cheese noodles, a donut, and decaf coffee.

My daily meds are Flomax, 0.4 mgs and Avodart 0.5 mgs for BPH before treatment with lots of water. Every other day after treatment, I had been taking Maxide, 12.5 mgs for hypertension.[31] I also take one Centrum Silver multivitamin tablet daily with breakfast.

---

movement. It also shows the busts of the four evangelists—Matthew, Mark, Luke, and John—fashioned by several other sculptors, Jill Burkee and Giancarlo Bingi.

[31] Avodart is a 5-Alpha-reductase inhibitor for treating benign prostate hypertrophy (BPH). https://www.health.harvard.edu>newsletter_article>B_t. Maxide is an oral diuretic which conserves Potassium used for treating Hypertension. https://

At the office, after responding to emails, I attended a conference on risk with the DOH risk manager and some other senior DOH staff.

I reviewed a PowerPoint presentation being prepared with the help of the fellow assigned to work with us here at APRA. I also completed a chronology of my involvement with the two mercury incidents, which the fellow would type for me to give to the DOH director.

I went to the noon mass at St. Aloysius Gonzaga Catholic Church,[32] a brisk, ten-minute walk from the office. I tried to walk there at least two or three times a week for the exercise, and I always prayed the rosary for many worldwide needs.

This reference was sited earlier as # 14.

I arrived home around 5:30 p.m. and found Shirley doing some paperwork in the living room.

There was the aroma of baked salmon in the air.

We have been without a kitchen floor for over three weeks since the leak from the filter system of the refrigerator being repaired by Sears is ongoing. Shirley has sent them three

---

www.webmd.com>drugs>maxide-oral>details. https://www.sciencemuseum.org.uk>medicine>bubon …

[32] en.wikipedia.org/wiki/Aloysious_Gonzaga. St. Aloysius Gonzaga was born March 9, 1568, and died on June 21, 1591 at age twenty-three from the bubonic plague caused by the bacterium *Yersinia pestis*. (yp) https://jmvh.org>article>the-history-of-the-plague-pF-2t. *Yersinia pestis* was named after the French bacteriologist Alexandre Yersin, who discovered the plague bacillus during the Hong Kong epidemic in 1894. St. Aloysius Gonzaga was canonized on December 31, 1726, by Pope Benedict XIII. His feast day is June 21, which is also my wife's birthday.

estimates of costs for the repairs, which required the flooring to be removed.

I changed into some sweats and tennis shoes and went to the basement and rode the stationary bike while praying four decades of the Joyful Mysteries of the rosary. Then I had a brisk walk around the basement with eight-pound weights in each hand in preparation for the upcoming tennis tournament I would enter.

After I showered, Shirley and I enjoyed the baked salmon along with a large salad with ranch dressing.

After dinner, we watched an old movie starring Edward G. Robinson, Nina Foch, and George McCready—*Johnny Allegro*—while I enjoyed a cold beer.

I stopped a few minutes before the movie ended and watched *24*. Shirley had fallen asleep about halfway through the movie.

I ended the evening with more reading of *Fatima, in Lucia's Own Words*.

March 7 is the feast day of Saints Perpetua and Felicity,[33] but the day being a Sunday, it is not celebrated.

---

[33] They were African Christian martyrs in the third century. Vibia Perpetua was an educated noblewoman with an infant, and Felicity was a slave who was pregnant at the time. Felicity delivered a child before she and Perpetua, whose father took her infant child, were led to the arena, mauled by animals, and eventually killed by a gladiator. Felicity's child was claimed by the Christians. They were proclaimed saints by the local bishop because they refused to deny their Christian faith. The proclamation as saints was via pre-congregation, appropriate at that time as there was no formal process for investigating the cause for sainthood. Their feast day was

Day 7
Tuesday, March 8, 2005

Awake about 5:45 am, I did some stretching exercises in bed and said some morning prayers. I had shaved the previous night, so I needed only to brush my teeth, shower, and dress.

The rain, very heavy, had started about 4:00 that morning with accompanying gusts of wind as forecast.

I left for the shrine about 6:20 and began the Sorrowful Mysteries also offering a few prayers to St. Joseph and Mother Mary Lange for special intentions.[34]

March 8 is the feast day of St. John of God, the religious founder of what is now the Brothers Hospitallers.[35] At one

---

proclaimed on March 7 by Pope Pius VI, the day they were martyred. https://www.catholic-org>saints>saint_id=48.

[34] Foley, OFM, Leonard, *Saint of the Day, Lives, Lessons and Feasts*. en.wikipedia.org>wiki>Mother_Mary_Lange. Mother Mary Lange was born Elizabeth Clarisse Lange in Santiago de Cuba, Cuba, in 1784, exact date not found. She died on February 3, 1882, in Baltimore at age ninety-eight. She was a Black Catholic religious nun who founded the Oblate Sisters of Providence in Baltimore in 1829, where she was named mother superior and took the name of Mary. The word *nun* comes from the Old English nunne and the Latin nonna "nun," originally a generic word for addressing an older person. https://www.vocabulary.com.dictionary.nun. https://wwww.dictionary>browse>nun. Nuns are women members of a religious order especially one whose members are bound by vows of poverty, chastity, and obedience. They generally work with the sick and elderly, some with orphans and providing schools for them. This was the first African American religious congregation, and they provided education for young black children and a home for the orphaned.

[35] en.wikipedia.org/wiki/John_of_God. Rudge, F. M., "Saint John of God—The Catholic Encyclopedia."

time, he was hospitalized for an acute mental illness, and after recovering, he began working with the mentally ill. He was reported to have had visions of the Virgin Mary and the Archangel Raphael. He died on March 8, 1550, and was canonized on October 16, 1690. He is the patron saint of nurses, hospitals, the mentally ill, and the dying.

Knowing that March 19 was the feast day of St. Joseph, I had been making a thirty-day novena, prayers for a special request, and dedicating the month to St. Joseph [36SJ]. I arrived at the shrine in time for the 7:00 a.m. mass. Having finished three decades of the rosary, I finished the fourth and fifth while driving to WHC.

After therapy, I noted softer stools and more flatus.

Treatment started at 8:20 a.m. and was completed by 8:27 a.m.

At the office, I read emails and set up some unread mail in a folder in archives to review later. I called Julian, the DOH risk manager, and we discussed some internal issues.

As I looked out the window around 10:30 a.m., the rain had turned into blustery white fluffs of snow blowing almost horizontally.

I had had my usual breakfast but no sausage. I have been saving my donut to eat at lunch as my dessert, which has worked out well.

Because of the outside weather conditions, I did not go to the noon mass today.

After lunch, I reviewed the Safety Plan with Valentina, one of the senior staff, who had essentially put the plan together.

All the policies and plans would need updating from the year 2000.

I left the office at 4:30 p.m. It was very windy and much colder. While walking across New York Avenue to the parking lot, I felt I was fighting thirty-mile-per-hour headwinds. I stopped by the shrine for the 5:15 mass.

The days are getting longer however, as I noted some sunshine as late as about 6:15 pm.

At nine, I was in bed reading some office stuff and some religious stuff. Shirley was already asleep.

[36,SJ] *The Mystical City of God, The Divine History and Life of the Virgin Mary*, by Venerable Mary of Agreda, Fiscar Marison Rev. Geo. J. Blatter, 1978; Charlotte, NC: Tan Books, 137–38, 2012.

It is recorded that the men who were descendants of the Tribe of Juda, of the race of David, were gathered together in The Temple. One would be selected by the High Priest to be the Spouse of the 14 year old Princess Mary. The High Priest placed a dry stick, a Staff, in the hands of the men, one of whom was Joseph of Nazareth, about 33 years old and known to be a ['just man']. They were commanded to ask, pray, as to which would be singled out to be the Spouse of Mary.

While all were in prayer, the stick, Staff, which Joseph held was seen to blossom and at the same time a White Dove rested on Joseph's head. Joseph, for his part, heard God say, "Mary shall be your spouse; accept her with attentive reverence, for she is acceptable in my eyes, just and most pure in soul and body and thou shall do all that she shall say to thee."

At this manifestation and token from heaven, the priests declared Joseph to be the spouse selected by God for the Maiden Mary.

Much of what is known about Joseph comes from the gospels of Matthew, Luke, and John. It is written that he died in the arms of Jesus and Mary. Joseph is venerated as St. Joseph in the Catholic Church, the Orthodox Church and Anglicanism, and patron of the Catholic Church. His feast days are March 19 and May 1.[36]

Day 8
Wednesday, March 9, 2005

I awoke at 5:30, stretched, and said morning prayers. After shaving and showering, I read some prayers to St. Joseph, Wednesdays being the day the Catholic Church dedicates to him.

The weather is still cold with blustery winds. I arrived at the shrine just in time for the 7:00 mass.

---

[36] Franciscan Media ISBN 978-0-86716-88-7, https://en.wikipedia.org/wiki/Saint_Joseph.

Today is the feast day of St. Frances of Rome,[37] born to a wealthy aristocratic family in Rome in 1384. At age thirteen, she was given in marriage by her parents, which she did not want but stayed in for forty-two years. She had a boy and two girls. The girls died at an early age, one due to the plague, rampant during that time.

She founded the Olivetan Oblates of Mary, and after her husband died, she moved into the monastery and became the group's president. Later, they became known as the Oblates of Saint Frances of Rome.

I started the Glorious Mysteries of the rosary, and by the time I had parked, checked in, and was on the treatment table, I was able to finish the fifth mystery, the Coronation of the Blessed Virgin Mary.

I had to stop by the men's room before reaching the treatment room and noted a soft brown stool.

After completion of the course of therapy, the same as usual, I checked out, dressed, and left for the office.

I stopped by McDonald's for a hotcake special—three hotcakes, scrambled eggs, sausage, hash browns, a carton of milk, and decaf coffee. For dinner the previous night, I had

---

[37] www.catholic.org/saints/saint/php?_id=49. "She was a Mystic with the gifts of miracles and ecstasy, of seeing her guardian angel, an Archangel, in bodily form on regular occasions, as well as revelations concerning Purgatory and Hell." She was canonized on May 9, 1649, and is honored as the patron saint of automobile drivers and of all Oblates.

had a sandwich of ham, turkey, and chicken and a large cup of butter pecan ice cream, so I was pretty hungry that morning.

I had taken my Maxide 12.5 mgs that morning, and while responding to my 144 emails, I noted for the first time the urgency to urinate and again about 10:00 a.m. with another soft brown stool.

I also reviewed a PowerPoint presentation to the staff.

I did not have any lunch following my big breakfast, and I did not go to noon mass.

At 1:40, I noted the need for another urgent bathroom call, and again, a soft stool, not loose. I was thinking about the frequency of urination and their relationship to the radiation therapy and my need to keep hydrated.

At 3:50 p.m., I noted the need for another bathroom visit and would have another soft brown stool. I made a note to discuss these with Dr. P in the morning.

I finished in the office around 4:45 and stopped by the shrine for the 5:15 mass, at which there were prayers to the Virgin Mary in the Miraculous Medal Novena.[38]

---

[38] en.wikipedia.org/wiki/miraculous_medal. "The Miraculous Medal is a devotional Medal, the design of which was originated by the Blessed Virgin Mary and told to St. Catherine Laboure at an apparition on November 27, 1830, in Rue du Bac, Paris, France. [Around the margins of the medal are the words "O Mary conceived without sin, pray for us who have recourse to thee."] Mary is standing on a globe in the center. On the reverse side is a circle of twelve stars and a large letter *M* surrounded by a cross and the heart of Jesus crowned with thorns and the Immaculate Heart of Mary pierced by a sword."

I cannot remember a time when I have not had a medal around my neck. The medal was fashioned after St. Catherine Laboure[39] was told to have the Miraculous Medal fashioned by The Virgin Mary. As a nun, she worked with the elderly and infirmed and is recognized as the patron saint of seniors. She was canonized by Pope Pius XII on July 27, 1947.

She was a French Catholic Daughter of Charity who cared for the elderly and infirmed who had an apparition of the Blessed Virgin Mary.

I had been in a car accident on February 7, 1999, and had sustained a concussion and lacerations of my scalp and hands, having been T-boned by an elderly man driving an old Cadillac. I woke up at WHC with a rosary and my Miraculous Medal on the side rails of my bed.

I was still practicing surgery at the time and had left the office at about 4:00 pm for a 4:30 appointment with Kim, a very talented and attractive female dentist, a periodontist,[40] for treatment of gum disease.

---

[39] en.wikipedia.org/wiki/Catherine_Laboure. St. Catherine was a French Nun of the Daughters of Charity born May 2, 1806, and died at age seventy on December 31, 1876. She had numerous apparitions with the Blessed Virgin Mary, the most significant of which is discussed above.

[40] www.perio.org>consumer>what-is-a-periodontist. A periodontist is a dentist who specializes in prevention, diagnosis, and treatment of periodontal diseases and provides implantation services.

I was driving north on Third Street NW past the Third and Van Buren tennis courts when I noted without turning my head that a car was coming. I thought, *is this guy going to stop at that stop sign?* I say "guy" reflexively; I did not know if the driver was male or female.

The speed limit in the area was twenty-five miles per hour. I remember the impact and my Chevy Blazer being pushed across the road. I was sliding in it upside down with my seat belt on.

A woman screamed, and I said, "Lady, you have to calm down. I need you to call my wife and tell her I've been in an accident"!

After all these years, I can recall quite vividly some of those events. I heard someone say, "Cut him out! Get him in for an MRI." I was admitted to the WHC in NW DC.

The magnetic resonance imaging (MRI) of my brain was negative, i.e., there was no evidence of bleeding or fracture or any other pathology.

I was essentially alert and reactive during the three days of conservative treatment and hospitalization. I was discharged on the third day.

As a surgeon, I was concerned about the concussion but also the lacerations on my hands, but fortunately, they were superficial and healed without any suturing.

The driver of the Cadillac, and elderly gentleman I was told, had not been injured thankfully.

After a month at home and successfully completing a series of post-event neuro-psychiatric evaluations, I was able to return to work.

Before I performed my first operation, I took a three-day course on minimally invasive surgery in Indianapolis, which included operating on pigs and testing the strength and flexibility of my hands and depth perception.

My first day back, I attended Mass at the shrine and got home around 6:30 p.m. The evening was again uneventful, and Shirley and I went to bed around 10:00.

Day 9
Thursday, March 10, 2005

This was my ninth day of therapy, but I have no documentation of the day's activities and therefore surmise that there were no unusual activities but Mass, routine office work, and a quiet evening at home.

THE JOHN CARROLL SOCIETY

HEALTH CARE AWARD

is presented to

Thomas J. Calhoun, M.D.

❧⤜⟶❧

for outstanding service to the
WASHINGTON ARCHDIOCESAN
HEALTH CARE NETWORK

MARCH 25, 2001

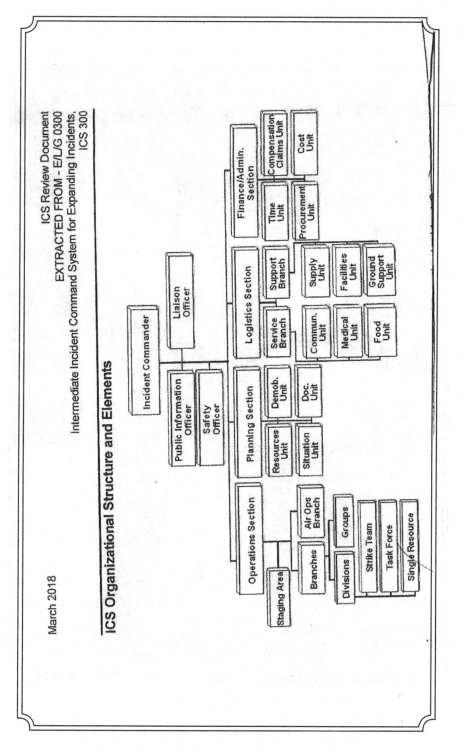

March 2018

ICS Review Document
EXTRACTED FROM - E/L/G 0300
Intermediate Incident Command System for Expanding Incidents,
ICS 300

ICS Organizational Structure and Elements

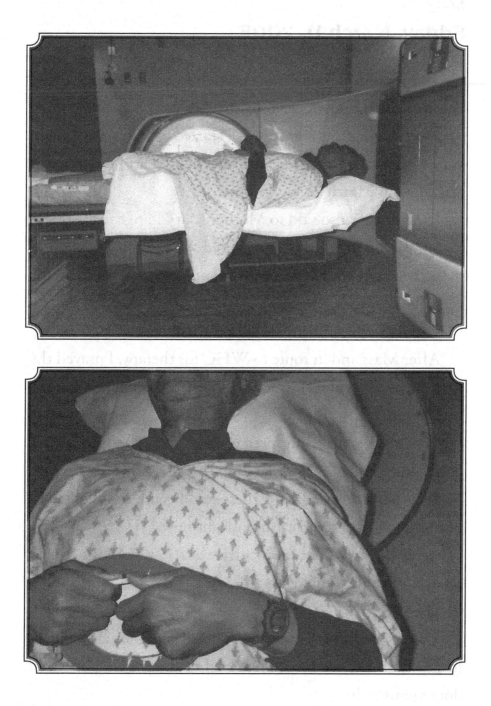

Day 10
Friday, March 11, 2005

Up at 5:15, did the usual exercises while praying seven Glory Be's dedicated to my guardian angel, G2.

After shaving and showering, I started prayers to St. Joseph as part of the nine-day novena I was making leading up to his feast day on March 19.

Prayers were also said to Mother Mary Lange for a special intention and for her being honored with the designation as blessed, a step toward canonization with sainthood in the Catholic Church.

I arrived at the shrine in time for the 7:00 mass.

After Mass and in route to WHC for therapy, I prayed the Joyful Mysteries and finished the last two decades as therapy was ongoing.

Overall, I was feeling pretty good; my appetite was still good, and I had no pain related to therapy; however, urinary urgency had increased, and there had been a few close calls needing to get to the bathroom right now!

After therapy, I got to my office at about 8:40. I had had a big dinner the previous night, so I had two donuts and a decaf coffee.

I responded to emails and reviewed the unusual incident forms that had come in overnight, these being internal documents only.

I attended the 5:15 p.m. mass at the shrine and got home around 6:30. Shirley was in the den watching the news.

I enjoyed a Sardine Salad; it still being Lent;[41] no meat on Fridays for Catholics.

We turned in around 10:00 pm.

Day 11
Saturday, March 12, 2005

I stayed in bed until 7:00 a.m., but I did do my exercises with stretches and prayed the Joyful Mysteries before getting up to shave and shower.

After feeding the birds, I left in time for the 8:00 mass at the shrine. After Mass, I prayed another rosary, the Luminous Mysteries of Light, and went downstairs for breakfast at the shrine's cafeteria and to read the *Washington Post*.

I got home around 10:30 am, put some clothes in the washing machine, and began organizing our papers for income tax filing. I had made an appointment with our agent at H&R Block for Monday, March 14.

I had not heard from my friend David, an attorney who lived a few blocks away, about playing tennis that night,

---

[41] en.wikipedia.org/wiki>Lent. www.usccb.org>prayer-worship>liturgical-yearv. "Lent is a solemn religious observance in the Christian liturgical Calendar that begins on Ash Wednesday consisting of 40 days of prayers, fasting, sacrifices and almsgiving, ending at the Easter Vigil, the Saturday evening before Easter Sunday."

which we had been doing for the past two Saturday evenings from six to eight, so I decided to take a nap.

I noticed that come the weekend, I seemed to be more fatigued, a side effect of radiation therapy, and I had been advised to get adequate rest.

Shirley woke me about 6:15 p.m. saying, "David's on the phone."

He was at the tennis courts and reminded me that the previous weekend, we had agreed that unless one of us made contact to the contrary, we were on from six to eight. I implored him to wait, and I quickly dressed and left for the courts.

Fortunately, the indoor courts at 16th and Kennedy were only a seven- or eight-minute drive from our home in Crestwood with no traffic lights in route. I arrived about 6:30, so we were able to get in a good hour and a half of play.

I lost both sets, 1–6 and the 10-point tie breaker 4–7.

I enjoyed playing because I needed the exercise, but I just was not into it, but I had no remorse from losing. *Fatigue from the therapy?* I wondered.

Back home, I showered and had a vodka and orange juice and dinner.

Shirley and I watched TV and turned in at 10:00. I slept soundly except for two occasions when I awoke having to urinate.

Day 12
Sunday, March 13, 2005

I was up at about 8:00 and did my exercises and said my morning prayers. The temperature was in the mid-thirties—still cold and windy.

I went outside to feed my bird friends and pick up the *New York Times* and the *Washington Post*. I had some decaf coffee and took my medications, Flomax, Maxide, Avodart, and a Centrum Silver multivitamin.

Shirley and I went to the 10:30 mass at our parish church, St. Thomas Apostle,[42] and were back home by noon having had more coffee and donuts and conversations in the church basement after Mass.

After mass I did spend some time on the stationary bike and exercised with the eight-pound weights.

The rest of the day was spent reading and praying more rosaries.

Since I was home, urinary urgency and frequency were easily addressed.

---

[42] www.learnreligious.com>who>saint>Thomas-thev. St. Thomas is reported to have been born sometime in the first century and was chosen by Jesus as a disciple and apostle and died on December 21, 72. He is also known as Doubting Thomas [Thomas also means Twins] because he would not believe Jesus had risen from the dead, asserting, "Unless I see the marks of the nails in his hands and put my fingers in the marks of the nails and my hand in his side, I will not believe." Sometime later, he did see Jesus, and Jesus invited him to do what he wished, after which Thomas did believe, asserting, "My lord and my God." His feast day is July 3.

Day 13
Monday, March 14, 2005

Monday morning started as usual; awake at 5:30 a.m., morning exercises including stretching, a shave and shower, then to 7:00 mass at the shrine.

Between the drive to WHC for therapy and to the office, I prayed the Joyful Mysteries with my rosary.

Work at the office was again reading and responding to emails and reviewing policies and unusual incidents.

About 11:45, I walked to St. Aloysius Church for the noon mass. The exercise is great as it will help me get in condition for the upcoming Men's 70 Singles Tennis Tournament since I have not had much time to practice.

The walk to church and back to the office allowed me to complete a decade of the rosary, and during Lent, that gave me a feeling of satisfaction and joy.

I left the office around 4:45 and was able to make the 5:15 mass at the shrine.

After Mass, I attended the quarterly board meeting of the DC Medical Society (DCMS) from 7:00 to 9:00 p.m. The newly appointed Director of the DCDOH, Dr. Gregg Payne, an emergency room physician, reported that there had been some mail contaminated with anthrax at the Brentwood post office in NE DC. This was the site of the initial anthrax event at which two postal employees had died from anthrax exposure in October 2001. (See newspaper articles.)

Because there was no confirmatory evidence of contamination at this time, DCDOH had not activated the Emergency Health and Medical Service Administration.

When Dr. Payne was made the Director of DCDOH, he elected to bring in his team, and I had been transferred, a lateral move to APRA, to supervise the physicians working there. I was very disappointed about the change in positions, but I reassured myself that nothing happened without God's allowing it.

I arrived at home by 10:00 p.m., and while watching the news on TV with Shirley and having a vodka and orange juice (having had dinner earlier at the DCMS meeting), I saw a report about the possible anthrax contamination.[43]

Shirley and I recalled the events of 2001 regarding anthrax, and I mused for a moment recalling that she would not open any mail we received for a few days for fear of anthrax.

I did not mention that to her.

I had a shower, and we were in bed by 11:00 p.m.

---

[43] wwwnc.cdc.gov>eid>article.

Day 14
Tuesday, March 15, 2005

The morning activities were almost routine that day until noon, when I got a call from Dr. Walter Faggett requesting assistance at DC General Hospital with dispensing prophylactic antibiotics.

Dr. Faggett was the Chief Medical Officer for the Department of Health, and a friend of Shirley and me; he had known Shirley from the tennis circuit before I met her.

Apparently, postal workers at the V Street NE DC branch were exposed to mail suspected of being contaminated. Dr. Payne had reported a possible exposure at the DCMS meeting the previous night, but no definite factual evidence was available at that time as I noted previously.

DC General Hospital [44] was the only public hospital in SE DC where many local practicing physicians were trained, but it was closed having discharged the last patient on June 24, 2001. The hospital was being used by DCDOH for emergency preparedness training and other activities.

The postal workers had reported that on March 10, they had been given information regarding "a concern" about possible contamination of mail at that site.

After a discussion with the Director of APRA, I reported to the DC General site about 1:10 p.m. and was given an

---

[44] https://www.washingtonpost.com>politics>2001/06/24.

update and a walk-through of the site. This brought back many memories; much of my training as a surgeon and where I taught many young surgery residents and medical students had been at DCGH. Moreover, it was there that as chief resident in surgery, we had treated a patient with a mega-hernia initially by giving him a Pneumoperitoneum[45] before surgical repair.

At approximately 3:30 p.m., ninety-four postal workers had been screened and provided prophylactic antibiotics (Doxycycline and Ciprofloxacin) for possible anthrax exposure. Three individuals were allergic to both antibiotics and were given an alternative drug instead. The prophylaxis was felt to be indicated because there had been a positive culture for anthrax from mail at the Pentagon.

I called Dr. Payne but could not reach him, so I assumed the position of on-site Director of Operations since I was quite prepared with my experience as medical director for EHMSA under the Incident Command System,[46] a standardized approach to the command, control and coordination of emergency responses.

I gave an update to the staff at 4:00 p.m. on site, after which I went to the Health Emergency Coordination Center

---

[45] "The Use of Pneumoperitoneum in the Treatment of Megaherniae," *JNMA* 66:16–18, January 1975.
[46] en.wikipedia.org>wiki>Incident_Command_System. "The Incident Command System (ICS) is a standardized approach to the command, control and coordination of emergency response."

(HECC) at DCDOH, where updated information was provided to EHMSA workers.

I got home around 7:00 and told Shirley about the activities of the day. I relaxed the remainder of the evening before retiring for bed.

From Wednesday March 16, 2005, therapy day 15, through Wednesday March 23, therapy day 20, my daily activities were essentially the same … morning exercises, mass, therapy, routine office work, evening mass, and home.

Each evening, I did spend time on my exercise bike and walking with the two eight-pound pounds weights in preparation for the upcoming Men's 70s Tennis Tournament to be played at the new indoor clay courts at the University of Maryland.

Day 21
Holy Thursday, March 24, 2005

I awoke about 6:15 am since the only Catholic service that day would be the Washing of the Feet. I did pray the Joyful Mysteries of the rosary. Before getting out of bed, I did my usual morning exercises and said the seven Glory Be's for the guardian angels.

I fed the birds on the way to WHC for therapy. I arriving there about 7:45 and was done at 8:18. I got a hotcake special at the McDonald's next to the office—three soft, fluffy hotcakes, eggs and sausage, a potato cake, low-fat milk (Yuk!), and decaf coffee.

This is day twenty-one of therapy, and except for my needing to urinate frequently, there have been no other significant symptoms. My appetite is still very good and my energy level still high.

Work was the same—reading and responding to emails … no further update on the anthrax situation.

I put in a leave slip for the next day, Good Friday, since things had been rather quiet all week.

There was to be an all-day conference on April 4, and we would have the first meeting of the newly formed safety committee on April 7.

I left the office at 3:00, went home, and put out the trash for Friday pickup.

Shirley decided not to go the Holy Thursday services stating she would watch the shrine's service on TV.

I arrived at St. Thomas about 7:30 p.m. and took a seat in the front row. The two front rows had been roped off for the twelve male "apostles," from the parish, six of whom were Latino males, who have been designated by the parish. The washing of our feet by the priests, duplicating the event of Jesus's washing the feet of the apostles, a traditional part of the Holy Thursday service, was a very humbling but joyful experience for me.

Services ended about 9:30 p.m. I stayed and prayed another rosary.

Back home, I had a ham and cheese sandwich and watched the news after which I turned in. Shirley was already fast asleep.

Day 22
Good Friday, March 25, 2005

Good Friday started about 5:05 with stretching and other morning exercises in bed and seven Glory Be's. Again, since there is no mass that day except for Good Friday services at 6:30 p.m., I did some more exercises when I got out of bed before shaving and showering.

I fed the birds and arrived at WHC around 7:45 a.m.

The check-in system involves a soft beeping sound and a red light after flashing my ID badge across the laser-housed box that lets folks in the treatment room know the patient has arrived.

The therapy is designed to give as little radiation as possible to the bladder and rectum; it concentrates the seven concentric rotations over the prostate starting posteriorly then three each on the right first, then left at positions 6, 4:30, 2, 12:15, 11:15, 9, and 7:30 on the clock.

After completion of treatment, I stopped by the cafeteria in the shrine for breakfast of eggs, a salmon cake (no meat on Fridays during Lent), half of a large Belgian waffle, milk, and decaf coffee. As I was on leave, I was able to leisurely read the *Washington Post*.

After breakfast, I stopped by the confessional to receive the Sacrament of Reconciliation, Penance, widely underused by many Catholics, for the forgiveness of sins. There were four priests available for Confession, so the wait time was not very long. I have to keep remembering how blessed we were to have the National Basilica knowing that many places throughout the world do not have priests available for weeks or even longer.

I went home and spent most of the day reading, praying, and getting a good workout on the exercise bike.

After I showered again and took a nap, Shirley and I left for Good Friday services at St. Thomas Apostle, a few blocks from the Zoo, for the 6:30 p.m. services. After that, we returned home and spent a quiet evening watching TV turning in around 10:00 p.m.

We had baked salmon and a large salad for dinner.

March 26, 2005
Holy Saturday

I stayed in bed until seven saying my morning prayers and doing some stretching exercises.

Since Shirley was still in bed, I decided to go to the shrine, where I prayed the Joyful Mysteries of the rosary in the upper church at the Chapel of Our Lady of the Rosary. After some additional prayers to St. Joseph, I went downstairs to the cafeteria and had breakfast—half of a Belgian waffle, eggs and sausage, milk, and decaf coffee—after which I read the *Washington Post.*

The weather was still on the chilly side, but I stopped by our daughter Maria's grave to offer some prayers.

Maria, our youngest daughter, age twenty-eight, had been killed by a hit-and-run driver in a big eighteen-wheeler as we found out on August 19, 2003, while she and our oldest daughter, Christine, were driving to Miami where Maria had enrolled in Barry College. Maria had been driving. (See image of Maria.) Christine sustained multiple soft tissue and cervical and lumbar spine injuries but miraculously survived the accident and is now completely well.

When I got home, Shirley and I had some general conversation.

I noticed of late that come the weekend, I seemed to need a midday nap, and since Dave and I were going to play tennis from six to eight that night, I thought a nap would be nice.

I awoke about 3:15 p.m., got dressed, and took some clothes to dry cleaners. Back home, I put on my tennis clothes and stopped by Popeye's for a bucket of mild chicken, two large red beans and rice, and six biscuits. I thought that would taste great after playing tennis with Dave, and some would be left over for Easter Sunday dinner.

Dave and I played two sets. I won the first 6–1, and at 5–all in the second set, we played a 10-point tie breaker, which I won 7–4!

After I showered and ate and enjoyed a vodka and orange juice, sleep came easily about 10:30 p.m. in part I am sure since I had won both sets of tennis.

March 27, 2005
Easter Sunday

Shirley and I attended the 10:30 a.m. mass at St. Thomas. We lingered a while afterward in the church basement for conversation, coffee, and donuts with other mass attendees.

The remainder of the day was uneventful for Shirley and me. We felt quite elated to have completed the forty days of Lent.

Day 23
Monday, March 28, 2005

Awake at 5:30 and proceeded with stretches and morning exercises after which I began the Joyful Mysteries.

As I was scheduled to play my first round of tennis at 10:00 a.m., I had shaved the previous night, so I had only to shower. I was dressed by 6:00.

The weather was still cold and rainy but not much snow.

I put on my tennis attire and two pair of athletic socks, then dark-gray corduroy pants, a dark, long-sleeved sweater, and a pullover sweater.

I left for the 7:00 a.m. mass at the shrine, leaving crumbs from the really good pound cake Shirley had made several days earlier for the birds.

After Mass, I finished the fifth decade of the Luminous Mysteries of Light.

I arrived for my therapy at 7:55 and dressed with the two gowns. There were three other Black men in the dressing room all for therapy for various forms of cancer.

Mr. B told me he had been there for three months of therapy and said that he was feeling much better than when he had started. Another gentleman had what appeared to be cancer of the larynx.

I was called in at 8:10 and was finished by 8:18; I prayed two decades of the rosary while completing therapy. I offered one decade for Pope John Paul II[47] and one decade for Terri Schiavo,[48] the young woman who was in a coma with a feeding tube but died thirteen days after the tube was removed.

After treatment, I got a copy of the *Washington Post* and ate breakfast in the cafeteria at the shrine—oatmeal, a pad of butter, milk, a donut, and decaf coffee. Along with breakfast, I took a Centrum Silver multivitamin and a 500 milligram

---

[47] en.wikipedia.org/Pope_John_Paul_II. Karol Josef Wojtyla was born on May 18, 1920, and died as Pope John Paul II on April 2, 2005. He was elected pope in 1978 and succeeded Pope John Paul I, who died after thirty-three days in office. He is recognized as helping end communist rule in his native Poland and the rest of Europe. He was the first pope to visit the White House in October 1979. I was privileged to see him with our young children, Tom Jr., Christine, and Kathy on this visit at the outdoor Mass in DC. Among a myriad of firsts was his denunciation of Mafia violence in Southern Italy and describing as genocide, the massacre of the Tutsis by the Hutu in the Catholic country of Rwanda. On May 13, 2014, he was shot by the assassin Mehmet Ali Agca with a Browning 9-mm semi-automatic pistol four times, one of the bullets perforating his colon and small intestine. He underwent five hours of surgery and had a temporary Colostomy performed. The assassin was captured the same day. After his recovery, and after the colon had been reconnected several months later, he met with the assassin in his prison cell and after a long private conversation forgave him. One of the bullets was placed in the crown of the statue of Our Lady of Fatima. Pope John Paul was canonized, declared a saint in the Catholic Church, on April 27, 2014, by Pope Francis.

[48] https://en.wikipedia.org.>wiki>Terri_Schiavo-Case. The issue was between the husband who, after the hospital staff had told him his wife was essentially in a vegetative state, wanted the feeding tube removed, and the parents who wanted the tube left in. There was no living will or advanced directive. The incident resulted in the making of a new law, the Terri Schiavo Law. An extended legal argument occurred about the decision to remove or not to remove the feeding tube. An autopsy revealed extensive brain damage, which helped the husband prevail, and the tube was removed.

Tylenol tablet. I have found that at my age, seventy-three, taking some form of painkiller before playing tennis made the aches and pains after the match much less. I also put a bit of Flexall 444 ointment on my right elbow, both shoulders, and knees.

I arrived at the tennis courts around 9:30. It had been raining all morning, so I left my brown leather jacket and my DOH ID badge in the car and put on my black trench coat.

In the dressing room, I did some stretching and bending at the waist and jogging in place. I reported to the check-in desk at 10:10 am, but no one from the tournament committee was present. I joined in the conversation with several other entrants. Several of us had been playing each other since the Men's 35 Singles forty years earlier.

My match started at approximately 10:20 a.m. after a six- or seven-minute warm-up. My opponent elected to receive and immediately broke my serve and held serve for 2–Love. His serve was not particularly overwhelming, but due to my lack of play, I made more errors.

My last tournament was in September 2004 at the Kappa Classics here in DC on the Trinity College Campus, where I won the Men's 70 Singles, 3–6, 6–3, 6–2. I cannot remember the name of my opponent.

This player hit a lot of *moon balls* and high lobs that landed on or close to the base line resulting in my having to return them from near the back wall of the court. He broke my serve again for a 3–love lead before I settled down and won six straight games for the first set, and moved to a 5–love lead in the second set before relaxing, knowing full well that could get me in trouble.

By that time, several onlookers had arrived and were watching our match. I sensed my opponent begin to draw strength from the crowd, and he won the next two games; the score then 5–2.

I settled down and proceeded to hold my serve at love winning the match 6–3, 6–2.

My next match was 9:00 a.m. the next day, but I asked for a 9:30 start explaining to the umpire my therapy circumstances. My treatment would not be over until approximately 8:25, after which I was scheduled to have a short meeting with Dr. P, so the 9:30 time was granted.

I proceeded to shower and left for the office, a twenty-five-minute drive. I was not winded at all, which sometimes followed a match. The two sets played in just over an hour had not been that tiring. It was the first real test of my stamina after twenty-three days of radiation therapy.

After getting a carryout plate of rice mixed with peas, vegetables, a baked chicken thigh, some hot sausages, a small salad with croutons, peach slices, and a drink, I checked in about 12:30.

I had forgotten that on Good Friday, actually on Holy Thursday, because I had taken Friday off, we were told that offices on the third floor would be painted.

The office was in complete disarray with computers and phones disconnected but with glistening new paint on the walls and ceiling.

After I ate my lunch, I asked one of the staff to help reconnect my computer and phone. I reviewed over a hundred emails I had received over the long weekend and discussed some of the unusual events that had come up with the staff; as the risk manager for APRA, I had to deal with them.

I left the office about 4:50 and arrived at the shrine for the 5:15 mass.

On reflection, I was thankful that I had not needed to go to the men's room during my tennis match and that I could indeed play. As I recalled about 5:00, I had not gone to the men's room since around 11:30 a.m., after my match.

Mass was in the upper church as it would be all week. The priests would wear white vestments during this Octave[49] of Easter.

---

[49] https://en.wikipedia.org>wiki>Octave_(liturgy). "Octave," which derives from the Latin *octova* or eighth, has two senses in Christian liturgical usage. In the first sense, it is the eighth day after a feast day, and it always falls on the same day of the week as the feast day itself. In the second sense, the term is applied to the whole period of eight days. In the Catholic Church, Christmas is the only other period during which an octave is observed.

The weather was beginning to clear when I left work; much of the eastern sky was becoming blue, and I wondered if there would be a rainbow. I had seen a double rainbow several months earlier. No rainbow appeared, but the sky continued to clear with mixed gray clouds and large patches of blue though the winds were still somewhat blustery.

After Mass, I stopped by the Rock Creek Cemetery, visiting with Maria and spent some time in prayer.

When I home Shirley was resting, so I made a large vodka and orange juice and watched the sports reports and the news. The sports event of the week was the NCAA basketball championships. I had been pulling for Kentucky to beat Michigan State, primarily because Tubby Smith was the African American coach at Kentucky and there had been very few African Americans in that position. Unfortunately, Kentucky lost.

There was still some leftover Popeye's chicken and red beans and rice. Shirley made a salad, and we had a nice dinner.

We watched my favorite TV show, *24*, after which I was feeling the activities of the day catching up with me. Knowing I had to get up early in the morning for therapy and my tennis match, I was in bed by 10:00 p.m.

I had to get up around 1:30 and again at 3:15 to urinate. I had begun to keep a bottle of Gatorade at bedside, so after urinating, I drank a few swallows before going back to sleep.

I neglected to note that at therapy today, one of the therapists took several pictures of me on the treatment table. (See photos.)

Day 24
Tuesday, March 29, 2005

Awake at 5:15 and did the usual morning exercises and prayed the seven Glory Be's. I had shaved the previous night, which saved me about six to eight minutes in the morning.

The weather was warmer but still with some drizzling rain.

I completed the nine-day novena to the Holy Spirit and would complete thirty days dedicated to St. Joseph the next day, March 30.

I had packed my tennis bag the night before with my tennis clothes under the dress clothes for the day. I wore black pants, a black EHMSA logo shirt, no tie, a green vest, and a gabardine sports coat with a figure of the guardian angel on the lapel.

I arrived at the shrine just in time for the 7:00 a.m. mass. Therapy did not start until 8:15, the one day I wanted to start early due to my match at 9:30, and was completed by 8:20.

I dressed to meet with Dr. P. Ordinarily, we were asked to keep our gowns on when we met with the physician, but as I had no complaints and was feeling good actually, and thinking about my 9:30 match, I was fully dressed when we met.

He told me he had driven to Florida for a week and had driven back in seventeen hours. He indicated that my lab findings were good as were my vital signs, and he encouraged me to continue the present course, now with only twenty days of therapy left. My blood pressures ranged between 147–150/84–86, my pulse was in the low to mid-eighties, and my appetite and energy were good.

I left for the courts and got there around 9:20. I had not taken my usual pre-match Tylenol, so I spoke with the person at the check-in desk and was given an Ibuprofen; no Tylenol was available. I had not eaten any breakfast, so I drank an Ensure Plus, a form of liquid nutrition supplying about 350 calories with a good amount of the seven dietary essentials—fats, carbohydrates, protein, minerals, vitamins, and electrolytes; water was the seventh, which was readily available at the courts. I also had a bottle of orange Gatorade at courtside from which I drank liberally on changing sides.

I did not have time to do as many warm up stretches as I wanted to but did check in at 9:30 and met my opponent, one of the seeded players.

I was a bit nervous, more than I had been for previous matches, and it was, I am sure, because I knew I was not really in tournament shape.

I broke his service to win the first game and then promptly lost my serve for 1–all. I would break him two more times but lost the first set 3–6. He won the second set 1–6, and the match was over in about an hour; but all things considered, I felt pretty good for having won one round. I believe that if I had been completely well, i.e., not having therapy, I could have won that match, but I surely would have won a set.

After showering and getting dressed, I felt whipped driving to the office I think more so due to the effects of the loss, not to the energy the match had required of me. I also felt that God willing, I could easily complete the next twenty days of therapy with lots more tennis tournaments ahead!

I arrived at the office around 11:45 and picked up some lunch—a cheeseburger and French fries. After lunch, I reviewed emails, put my office furniture back in place, and put up my certificates, which had been taken down for painting.

I finished in the office around 4:30 and left for the pharmacy at Providence Hospital for refills I had to pick up before five o'clock. I then attended the 5:15 mass at the shrine. I stopped by the cemetery and offered some prayers at Maria's grave, that time praying the Chaplet.[50]

---

[50] https://.www.simplycatholic.com>what-is-Chaplet. "A Chaplet is a personal devotional prayer that can be prayed privately or in a Group, quietly or out loud, silently, in a Church or in an ordinary setting." Https://en.wikipedia.org>wiki. Chaplet_of_the_Divine._"A form of Christian prayer which uses prayer beads similar to, but distinct from the Rosary."

I remembered that we were low on bread and juice, so I stopped by the 14th Street Giant's Food and picked up a few things. I got home around 6:45 in time for the news.

Shirley and I had dinner—chicken, potatoes and gravy, and a salad.

By 9:30, I was pretty tired. I realized I was replaying points from my match thinking if I had done this or that I could have won. That, however, was a no-win situation, so I said some prayers and fell asleep around 10:00 p.m.

Day 25
Wednesday, March 30, 2005

Awake at 5:15 and proceeded with the usual morning exercises and prayers. After shaving and showering, I dressed and offered some special prayers for our children, Tom Jr., Christine, and Kathy, that they be given the gifts of Understanding, Counsel, Knowledge, Wisdom, Fortitude, Piety, and Fear of the Lord, which the Catholic Church recognizes as the Seven Gifts of the Holy Spirit.

Since they had been baptized and confirmed in the Catholic Church, they had already received these blessings, but like many of us, they had not acknowledged and accepted these gifts.

I arrived at WHC and started therapy at 8:12, again finishing at 8:19.

After dressing and heading to the office, I stopped at the McDonald's for a hotcake special, milk, and decaf coffee. While eating breakfast, I reviewed emails and the safety policies and past emergency preparedness responses for APRA. In addition to being the risk manager for APRA, I am also responsible for emergency preparedness and performance improvement, each area quite demanding.

Because APRA's clientele were individuals with substance abuse issues, the Emergency Preparedness Response Policy required a great deal of input from the Mental Health Department, so it was good working with them.

About 12:30, since I had missed the noon mass at St. Aloysius, I went out for a short, snappy walk during which I prayed the Luminous Mysteries. I stopped at a food cart for a hot dog with mustard, relish, and onions and a root beer for lunch.

Back in the office, I continued with polices and email reviews and left the office around 4:45pm, then I attended 5:15 mass at the shrine.

At home, after dinner, Shirley and I watched TV and talked about our day. She went to bed at nine while I stayed up and watched the ten o'clock news, after which I went to bed.

Because I was having more urinary frequency due to the therapy, I had been sleeping in the room where my office was so as not to disturb Shirley by getting out of bed so often.

From Thursday, March 31, day 26, through April 12, day 35, 2005, there were no unusual events. Radiation therapy was each weekday as previously noted, and daily routines were as noted—morning prayers and feeding the birds on the way to the 7:00 mass at the shrine, breakfast from McDonald's, and on to the office, with mass after work at the shrine.

Work was ongoing with the Department of Mental Health for policies that would become a part of DOH's All Hazards Emergency Response Plan.

Shirley and I attended the 10:30 Sunday mass at our parish church, St. Thomas Apostle, while Saturday and the evenings were uneventful.

It had been a little over a month since I had started therapy, and the only symptoms I had were urgency, frequency of urination and some afternoon fatigue.

Day 35
Monday, April 13, 2005

Awake at 5:45 and performed morning exercises and said morning prayers. I had a somewhat restless night but was not sure why.

I shaved, showered, and dressed. The mornings were still a bit chilly, so I put on my corduroy pants, a vest over my white collarless shirt, my black and tan scarf, and the brown leather flight jacket, and left for the 7:00 a.m. mass at the shrine, of course feeding the birds in route to the car.

April 13 is the feast day of Pope St. Martin I, the last pope to have died a martyr.[51]

After Mass, I stopped by Our Lady of Lourdes Chapel and prayed the first three decades of the Joyful Mysteries and then left for therapy.

The day was treatment cycle number 4 in the Alpha Room, but after a few minutes, I noted the machine had stopped. After several buzzing sounds unlike any I had previously heard, a technicians told me, "The two computers aren't talking to each other, so we'll have to move you to the Beta Room" just a few feet away for completion of my therapy.

Of all days for that to happen when I had told Sharon I would pick up a document from her at 8:45 a.m. when I came to the office. Sharon had been working with me for the previous six months to complete the final report on the DC Lead crisis. In February 2004, the *Washington Post* reported there had been an increased amount of Lead in DC's drinking water.

After five months of community outreach, multiple in-office discussions, educational presentations to senior citizens' organizations, multiple city council hearings and blood lead levels being obtained from over 6,800 DC residents from age six months to eighty-four years, no health issues were

---

[51] *Catholic Encyclopedia*, Pope Saint Martin I.

documented as being related to the elevated Lead levels.[52] The acceptable Lead level established by the Environmental Protective Agency (EPA) is 15 parts of Lead per billion. This is not a health parameter according to the EPA but an "action" level that if exceeded would prompt additional water purification efforts.

Two young African American males had been hospitalized with Lead levels above 45 micrograms per deciliter; however, they lived in houses with Lead-based paint and plaster and had ingested some plaster over time according to their medical history.

We at the DCDOH were privy to this information out of concern for the safety of DC residents.

Preliminary findings were published by the Centers for Disease Control and Prevention (CDC) in an article on March 30, 2004 as noted below. When the final report is completed about the experiences here in DC, it may well be a landmark reference for other health care workers.

I called Sharon at 9:15 to let her know I was running late, but as it turned out, her voice mail said she had been delayed at a meeting and would call me later.

---

[52] "Blood Lead Levels in Residents of Homes with Elevated Lead Levels in Tap Water—District of Columbia, 2004: Morbidity and Mortality Weekly Report" Dispatch, vol. 53, 3/30/04.

The Beta Room was a mirror image of the Alpha Room in which I usually received my therapy, so cycles 5 through 7 were given in the Beta Room.

I drove to the office and stopped at the McDonald's for a hotcake special, milk, and decaf coffee. Dr. P had recommended that I drink cranberry juice to address my urinating frequency, and at lunchtime, I did get a bottle of cranberry juice.

At 11:00 a.m., Dr. Gonzales (She has given me permission to use her name), the Chief of DOH's Emergency Medical Service (EMS), called to say that there was a bomb scare at Buildings 825 and 941, NE Capitol Street. Building 825 was the headquarters of DOH and 941 was the main DC tax office; they are directly across from each other.

When I arrived at Building 821 approximately fifteen minutes after I was notified, Dr. Walt Faggett, DOH's Chief Medical Officer, was there as were numerous police and fire department personnel. He quickly brought me up to date on what was known at that time. We participated in floor-to-floor inspections to make sure everyone had evacuated the buildings.

In Building 941, I had to show my police badge to an African American male who indicated he was a supervisor and had just started a meeting and was not leaving. I convinced him that multiple police would be available if he did not leave immediately.

He and the other workers promptly left!

We searched for several hours and found no bomb, only much anxiety having been created.

We had a *"hot wash"*, a brief meeting of the staff involved, at the main office, and then I left for my office. Final reports would be generated and submitted to the DOH director later.

Earlier in the day, I had called my agent at H&R Block from our home on NW Argyle Terrace to tell her I would be dropping off some items for completion of our 2004 taxes. I left home about 6:10 p.m. for the Tax office on NW Connecticut Avenue, but traffic was so bad that I called her and told her I would bring the information the next morning. I made that decision because thus far, I had not had to wear Depends, nor did I want to, and I did not want to take the chance that I would be caught up in the traffic needing to find a men's room.

It had been explained to me by my medical team and in pamphlets that these symptoms were to be expected during the late phase of radiation therapy.

The evening's activities were uneventful, and I was in bed by 10:00.

From April 14 through April 23, weekday activities included therapy and weekend rest, reading, and Mass on Sundays with Shirley.

Dave and I had stopped our Saturday tennis dates several weeks earlier, after I had played in the tournament.

I did take my tax information to H&R Block on April 14 to be submitted electronically by April 15.

Saturday April, 23, 2005

I woke up about 6:15 having slept through most of Friday night.

I had been keeping a large bottle of cranberry juice and another of water at bedside so I could keep tanked up what with my having to urinate frequently.

After the usual morning exercises and prayers, I went to the 8:00 mass at the shrine after which I prayed the Joyful Mysteries on this sixth day of the nine-day novena to the Holy Spirit and to St. Anthony of Padua.[53] I noted that I had been able to stay through Mass and prayers without having to go to the men's room, a blessing I ask for at each Mass.

I went downstairs to the cafeteria, where a large tour group visiting the shrine was, and by the time I got in line for breakfast, all the sausage and bacon as well as pancakes

---

[53] en.wikipedia.org?wiki>Anthony_of_Padua. St. Anthony of Padua, a Doctor in the Catholic Church, was born in Lisbon, Portugal, on August 15, 1195, and died on June 13, 1231, at age thirty-five in Padua, Italy, where today a large basilica in his honor is located. He was canonized on May 30, 1232, by Pope Gregory IX, one year after his death. "He is especially invoked and venerated all over the world as the patron Saint for the recovery of lost items and lost spiritual goods."

were gone. I tried to maintain a Christian attitude when I noticed a guy in line two places ahead of me with three links of sausage ... How dare he? I found out later that the group was visiting from Utah, and I welcomed them to DC.

After reading the *Post*, en route to my car, I met Monsignor R, who a few weeks earlier had been appointed the director of the Basilica of the Shrine of the Immaculate Conception, and I offered him my best wishes. Before he was made a monsignor, he was one of the priests who concelebrated the funeral mass for our daughter Maria on September 9, 2003, at our parish church, St. Thomas Apostle. His new position was a surprise for Shirley and me but a special blessing indeed from our Lord!

Maria, the youngest of our four children, was special indeed. There is no doubt in my mind that the youngest child is often more innovative, perhaps for just having to find his or her place in the family structure. Shirley was often disabled during Maria's early teen years, and Tom Jr., Christine, and Kathy were away in college.

As a solo general surgeon, I was working seven days a week often in the operating room late hours or early morning hours, so my input at the home was spotty, not for a lack of desire on my part but because of the circumstances.

I noted Maria had developed a slight stammer. She was enrolled at Georgetown Visitation School, an academically oriented all girls' Catholic school in DC, and this was becoming more and more an academic challenge for her. On more than one occasion, she asked us to transfer her to Alice Deal, a public elementary school as several of her friends had done, and at which Shirley had taught.

After school, Maria was responsible for tending to many of Shirley's needs until I got home. We had several women as housekeepers, but their reliability and compatibility were frequent challenges.

Maria and Tom Jr. were the best athletes of the children, and Maria could throw overhand naturally after just a few lessons from Shirley when she was up and about. Shirley also taught her how to hit a strong, coordinated serve. (See image of Maria serving.)

After deliberation, we did transfer Maria to another school, and she graduated from Emerson High School in northwest DC with no stammering and feeling very good about school.

After graduation, she moved in with her friend Joe, a decision Shirley and I did not initially agree with, but she was eighteen then, so we reluctantly agreed.

During this time, she was awarded a tennis scholarship to Howard University playing on the team with one of the Williams sisters.

After a year at Howard, she worked as a live-in dorm mother and assistant tennis coach at Madeira, the all-girls' school in McLean, Virginia. (See image of Maria Teresa Calhoun.)

Over three hundred attended Maria's funeral mass; Madeira closed for a half-day, and many of the girls and staff were present.

I got home around noon, and as the weather was overcast and cool, I decided to take a nap. My need to nap had been foretold to me by my radiation therapy staff as I got into the late phases of treatment.

The remainder of the day, weekend actually, was uneventful.

Sunday, April 24, 2005

Shirley and I went to Mass at St. Thomas, and after coffee and donuts and conversation after Mass, we spent the remainder of the day relaxing.

Day 41
Monday, April 25, 2005

Awake at 5:45 and performed the usual morning exercises and prayers followed by a shave and a shower.

The weather was still un-spring like; the weather report had said the day would be in the low to mid-thirties.

I attended the 7:00 mass at the shrine. It was the feast day of St. Mark the Evangelist,[54] whose gospel is the shortest and the only one I had read in its entirety.

I said a few prayers in route to therapy. After registering and proceeding to the treatment room, I greeted Mr. B, who was the only other person present. Shortly thereafter, another patient arrived for treatment and was called to start his treatment. That caused Mr. B to ask no one in particular, "What's going on? I was here before him."

By 8:20, I had not been called, and soon thereafter, one of the therapists told Mr. B and me that the computer in the Alpha Room was not working properly and that was why there were delays. Eventually, we did have our treatment in the Beta Room.

After parking at the office, I got breakfast at the McDonald's that I took to my office.

I went to the noon mass at St. Aloysius as I had a Board meeting at 6:00 p.m. at the DC Medical Society, and would not be able to attend at the shrine.

I was home around 9:30, and after Shirley and I discussed our day, I showered and was in bed by 10:30.

---

[54] https://en.wikipedia.org/wiki/Mark-the-Evangelist. St/ Mark was born in AD 5 in Cyrene, Pentapolis, of North Africa. His is the shortest of the four gospels. He is reported to "have a rope around his neck and dragged by pagans through the streets of Alexandria until he was dead." His feast day is April 25. He is the patron saint of lawyers, pharmacists, and lions—yes, lions!

Day 42
Tuesday, April 26, 2005

Nothing unusual today, morning exercises, prayers, 7:00 mass at the shrine, breakfast from McDonald's, review of emails, and the 5:15 p.m. mass at the shrine before heading home.

I was in bed by 10:00 knowing that the next day was day forty-three, the last day of therapy.

Day 43
Wednesday, April 27, 2005

Completion day started in the usual way; awake at 5:30 with morning exercises, stretching, and morning prayers, then shaving and showering and off to Mass at the shrine having dropped some bread crumbs for the birds on the way.

I am especially thankful to the good Lord for this day, forty-three days of radiation therapy. I can honestly say that I had not had a bad day. I had not had to take any sick leave, and I was able to win a round in a major tennis tournament. I could not help but feel good!

Will there be long-term negative effects? Well, bring them on!

At the end of the treatment session and meeting with the medical team, I received an unexpected surprise—a certificate for completion of the therapy. (See copy of certificate.)

My final activity was to proceed to the second floor for a final set of blood tests, a copy of which would be sent to my primary care doctor.

Tennis has been a major part of my life since age fourteen, when I won the first tournament I played in, the Florida State Juniors for Negroes (Colored) in Daytona, Florida.

Earlier, my best friend Jenk, Wilbur H. Jenkins Jr., also fourteen, and I had noticed two pretty girls playing tennis, and we were duty bound to meet them. We were playing basketball at the time, with no interest in tennis as it was thought of as a sissy game not played by boys.

The three white beach sand tennis courts were a part of the park and directly behind the basketball court. On other occasions, we had noticed several boys about our age playing and several adults, one of whom was General "Chappie" James, a colored air force member of the Tuskegee Airmen, we would learn, and another, "Chip" Reed, the playground director who was primarily responsible for my continuing to play tennis, and who took me to the junior boys' tournament in Daytona.

We introduced ourselves and later were invited to their home.

They lived in the section of town in Jacksonville, Florida, called Sugar Hill, where upper-class Negroes lived—lawyers and doctors.

It was at their home that Jenk and I saw our first TV show, in black and white.

We did not see the girls again, but Jenk and I developed a love and expertise for tennis that we played into our late eighties.

We enrolled as freshmen at Florida A&M College in 1950 in Tallahassee and played on the tennis team, me in the number 5 singles spot, Jenk number 6, and we were the number 4 doubles team.

Jenk withdrew from school and spent four years in the Air Force, much of it in Germany during which time his tennis skills improved markedly.

I was blessed to have received a tennis scholarship for my junior and senior years during both of which I was the captain of the team.

I was further blessed to have won the National Intercollegiate Singles Championships for Negro Colleges in August 1953. (See photo of award).

At that time, segregation and Jim Crow laws were in full force in the country, and we Colored, or Negroes, were not allowed to play in White tournaments.

It was at the ATA Nationals at Wilberforce, Ohio, in 1964 that I met Shirley Jones from Charlestown, West Virginia, who was playing in the women's semifinals, and we were married three years later on Saturday December 2, 1967.

On Thursday, December 2, 2021, we celebrated our fifty-fourth wedding anniversary with a Nuptial Mass.

Jenk became one of the first Negro men to play in the United Stated Lawn Tennis Open Tennis Tournament in Forrest Hills, New York City, in 1957, the year Althea Gibson became the first Negro female or male to win the tournament. He went to Saint Louis University on a partial tennis scholarship and the GI Bill, and after graduation, he attended Howard University Law School in DC, from which he also graduated in 1967.

Jenk and I were finalists in the American Tennis Association (ATA) National Men's Doubles five times winning the title in 1958 and 1960. We played in the Men's 80 Doubles finals at the hundredth anniversary of the ATA in Baltimore on August 4, 2017, losing to Walter Moore and Leon Bowser, 5–7, 0–6.

I had been training for this event for several months, but in the spring of 2017, my PSA was noted to be 16 ng/mL. Upon discussion of this finding with my urologist, Dr. Gerald Batipps (He has given me permission to use his name), we decided that I should be treated with Lupron,[55] a type of hormone therapy for prostate cancer. It worked by lowering the amount of testosterone, which helped slow the growth of the cancer cells. I had one injection, and I noticed that it did make me weaker, so I did not have any further therapy.

---

[55] https:www.medicalnewstoday.com>articles

As I noted in the dedication, Jenk died from metastatic prostate cancer on July 8, 2020. Several of our tennis buddies, Clyde, who was an ob-gyn surgeon, Paul, who taught adult education in DC, Jim, a tennis entrepreneur, Oswald, a thoracic surgeon, Aaron, a urologist and Henry, the pastor of a large Christian Church and a close childhood friend of ours in Jacksonville, Florida, all African American males, died of prostate cancer.

Jamie, who lived next door when we were children, now eighty-nine and still living in Jacksonville, had radium seeds implanted in his prostate in 2008 as treatment for prostate cancer. We talked on the phone on October 5, 2020, a day before my eighty-ninth birthday, October 6, 2021, and we agreed that we were blessed and felt pretty good at being above ground.

Jamie has given me permission to use his name.

I hope that all men starting at age forty-five regardless of socioeconomic status or occupation will in addition to seeing their primary physicians at least annually will visit with a urologist so that in the end, as my roommate in medical school, Dr. Francis Greene (He has given me permission to use his name), a urologist, told me, "They will die *with* prostate cancer, not *from* it."

The last part of the book will be a discussion on the prostate gland, which I hope will help demystify this most important gland for the non-health care individual.

The prostate is a firm, partly glandular and partly fibromuscular body located at the beginning of the urethra in the male. (See image of the prostate.)

Embryologically, it arises during the third month from the proximal part of the Urethra, from some earlier outgrowths, which are at first solid, then branch and become tubular.[56]

Similar outgrowths occur in some females but become rudimentary and are homologous to the prostate.[57]

In the female, these structures are Skene's glands (SG), referred to by some as the female prostate, discovered by Alexander Skene in the 1880s.[58]

The Prostate is about 4 centimeters from the Rectum, the lower part of the large bowel, somewhat conical (walnut) in shape. It has a base, an apex, posterior and anterior surfaces, and it is the base that presents for digital rectal exams.

Anatomically, according to Wikipedia, the prostate is divided into four lobes, anterior (in front), posterior (behind), lateral (to the side), and median (in the middle) The following quotes are from the Wikipedia article.[59]

The word prostate, is from the Greek-prostates, literally, one who stands before, protector, guardian.

---

[56] The prostate was first formally identified by Venetian anatomist Niccolo Massa in 1536. https://en.wikipedia.org>wiki>Prostate

[57] *Gray's Anatomy*, 35th British Edition, 190–91, Warwick and Williams, W. B. Saunders, Philadelphia, 1973.

[58] https://amsny.org>discovery>skenes_gland.

[59] http://74.125.95132/search?q=cache:tCqa-_gltn4J:en.wikipedia.org/ …

The main function of the prostate is to store and secrete a slightly alkaline (pH 7.29) fluid, milky or white in appearance, that usually constitutes 25–30% of the semen, along with spermatozoa and seminal fluid.

The prostate also contains some smooth muscles that help expel semen during ejaculation (Latin, verb, to eject a fluid e.g., semen).[60]

To work properly, the prostate needs male hormones (androgens) which are responsible for male sex characteristics.

The main male hormone is testosterone, produced mainly by the testicles, and small amounts by the adrenal glands.

A healthy prostate is slightly larger than a walnut and structurally can be divided in two different ways, by zones or lobes.

The *zone* classification is more often used in Pathology and the *lobe* in anatomy.

The prostate is subject to many clinical diseases such as Acute and Chronic Inflammation, Prostatitis, Impotence, Benign Prostate Hyperplasia or BPH, which is an enlarged prostate and Cancer.[61]

From the above references, we note, ([59, 61]) prostate cancer is the second leading cause of deaths from cancer among

---

[60] *Webster's All-In-One Dictionary & Thesaurus*, Springfield, MA: Federal Street Press, 2010.

[61] ([60a]https://zerocancer.org>…Am I at Risk?
http://www.medicinenet.com/prostate_/page 13.htm#_Toc4984 …
[61b] http://www.webmd.com>Prostate Cancer Guide.

men. There are no known specific measures to prevent the development of prostate cancer, nor are there any specific prostate cancer genes identified and verified to date.

African American men have the highest incidence of prostate cancer with one in seven more likely to get it, the reasons remain unclear. [60a]

Studies show that [data from prostate cancer biometrics are still preliminary and non-conclusive.][62]

If a biopsy is done and the diagnosis is prostate cancer, a number of therapeutic measures are available. These will be determined by the clinical stage and grade of the cancer, findings which will be discussed by the urologist and/or oncologist (cancer specialist).

Early diagnosis of prostate cancer can be made by yearly digital rectal exams (DRE) beginning at age 40 and yearly PSA testing beginning at age 50. [61b, 62]

Research in humans and animals has suggested that low fat diets and avoiding red meat may slow the progression of prostate cancers.

Environmental factors such as cigarette smoking and industrial toxins may promote the development of prostate cancer but these have not been clearly identified.

An article in the *AARP* magazine[63] suggests that leafy greens such as spinach and collards, cooked tomatoes or

[62] Int. J. molSci.20021 Apr., 22 (9): 4367.doi:10.3390/ijms22094367.

[63] *AARP*, June /July 2019, vol. 62, no. 4c, 20–22.

tomato sauce, citrus fruits, swapping butter for olive oil, and unfermented soy foods such as soy milk, tofu and edamame[64] may be associated with a significant decreased risk for getting prostate cancer.

Early symptoms of prostate cancer are much the same for BPH, including frequent urination, pain in the lower back, hips, upper thighs, loss of appetite, loss of weight, painful ejaculation and blood in the urine (Hematuria).[65]

If painful ejaculation and/or hematuria are noted, this should prompt an urgent visit to a urologist.

In addition to the digital rectal exam and PSA test noted above, routine blood tests, Urinalysis, Sonogram and possibly a Bone Scan, Computerized Axial Tomography (CT) or Magnetic Resonance Imaging (MRI) studies may be recommended.

To help determine if there is metastasis or spread of the primary prostate cancer to other organs, a Positron Emission Topography Scan (PET) may be indicated.[66]

Other tests now available are the ExoDx Prostate Test, or EPI, a simple, noninvasive urine test that can help determine if a biopsy of the prostate is indicated (exosomedx.com), the

---

[64] edamame is a plant-based type of soybean, a source of potentially heart protective Omega-Omega-3 fatty acids called alpha-linoleic acids and other nutrients such as fiber, vitamin C, calcium, iron, and proteins. info@everydayhealth.com, may also play a role in decreasing the risk of prostate cancer.

[65] urologyhalth.org/urologic-conditions/prostate-cancer.

[66] Hell J Nudmed, Sep-Dec 2020 (3):339345.doi:10.1967/s002449912211.

PCA3, a urine test for the prostate cancer gene 3 and the Prostate Health Index (phi), a blood test. (The latter two may be reviewed in menshealth.com/health/a25572821/prostate-cancer-screening-new-better-test.)

The PSA is a specific protein produced by the prostate gland referred to as a biological or tumor marker. It is a blood test measured in nanograms as PSA per milliliters (ng/ml). The PSA was discovered by a pathologist, Dr. Richard J. Ablin, and colleagues in 1970.[67]

Some physicians consider a PSA of 4.0 ng/ml or below as normal, but some studies have shown a diagnosis of prostate cancer in 15.2 percent of men with levels of 4.0 ng/ml or below.[68]

Several risk factors increase the likelihood of prostate cancer, including age; about 63 percent of cancer occurs in men aged sixty-five or older, family history, a father, brother and possibly diet.[69],[69a]

[69a]urologyhealth.org/urologic-conditions/prostate-cancer.

There are false positive results, i.e., the test is positive but no cancer is detectable.[70]

---

[67] https://pubmed.ncbi.ncm.nch.gov>.

[68] Thompson, I. M., Pauley, D. K., et al. "Prevalence of prostate cancer among men with a prostate specific antigen level of < or equal to 4.0 ng/ml." *NEJM* 2004:350 (22):2239–46.

[69] http://seer.cancer.gov/csr/1979, 2005/index.html. Last indexed from internet March 18, 2009.

[70] *Epidemiology*, 2nd ed., Leon Cordis, W. B. Saunders, 2000, 65–66, 68.

Some studies show that only 25–35 percent of men who have a biopsy due to an elevated PSA are found to have cancer of the prostate.[71]

A discussion with a urologist or oncologist should be had about the various tests and therapy available. Staging and the grade of the cancer helps determine the therapy recommended, which may be localized or systemic. Localized therapy includes surgery, radiation, cryotherapy, or focal therapy. Systemic therapy may be chemotherapy, hormonal or immunotherapy. Active surveillance should also be discussed.

This book will not attempt to address all diseases of the prostate or their diagnosis and treatment, but because I have BPH and prostate cancer, my emphasis has been on these two.

My biopsy results revealed Adenocarcinoma Gleason's Score 5 with a Clinical Stage 1. Gleason scoring was devised by Dr. Donald F. Gleason in 1962. It is a pathologic system with scores from 2 to 10 with the higher number indicating a greater risk and higher mortality of patients with prostate cancer.[72]

There are two main classification systems for staging prostate cancer. One is the tumor, node, metastasis (TNM) classification developed in the 1940s by Pierre Denoix.[73]

---

[71] Smith, D. S., Humphrey, P. A., et al., "The Early Detection of Prostate Cancer with Prostate Specific Antigen: The Washington University Experience." *Cancer* 1997; 80(9): 1853–56.

[72] https://en.wikipedia.org/wiki/Gleason-grading-system.

[73] https://www.ncbi..nim..nih/govarticles>PMC1329448.

Stages are described as 0, I, II, III and IV in keeping with the Union for International Cancer Control terminology.[74]

The other system is the American Urologic Staging system. These stages are A, B, C, and D with D1 designating spread of the malignancy to nearby or local lymph nodes and D2 to distant spread or metastasis to bone or liver.[75]

The author hopes that by the time this book is published, God willing, there will have been significant advances in prevention, diagnosis, and treatment of diseases of the prostate and mental and physical diseases overall.

On September 9, 2021, cancer.net/cancer-types/prostate-cancer/types-treatment, reports an excellent update, I think, about prostate cancer.

Up-to-date information about prostate cancer can be obtained at the Prostate Cancer Foundation (phone 301–570–4700) and American Cancer Society (1–800–ACS–2345).[76]

---

[74] https://www.uicc.org.

[75] http://www.medicinenet.com/prostate_cancer/page6.htm#_Toc4978 …

[76] htts://www.pcf.org/v. cancer.org/cancer/prostate-cancer/detection-diagnosis-staging.htm.

ABOUT THE AUTHOR

The author was born in Marianna, Florida, on October 6, 1932, to Sylvia Barnes, a young unwed colored female. The birth certificate indicates the father was J. R. Borders, whom the author never met.

His mother told him years later when he asked who J. R. Borders was, "He was just a friend."

He asked about his name, and she related he was named after his uncle, Tom Calhoun.

She said that one evening after returning home from picking cotton, she found me crying and in a soiled diaper with flies all around. The next day, she left with me on a bus for Jacksonville, Florida, to stay with her uncle and aunt, Tom and Luella Calhoun. They had given birth to twins who had died soon after birth and had no other children, so I was given to live with them.

It was not uncommon at that time for a child from families with several children to give one of them to a family with few children to help out on the farm.

His early training and education were at St. Pius Catholic School in Jacksonville, where he was an altar boy. He was taught by strict Catholic nuns from the Sisters of Saint Joseph and Jesuit priests.

He graduated from Florida A&M University in Tallahassee as a second lieutenant in the Reserve Officers Training Corps.

He was captain of the tennis team his junior and senior years.

After two years in the army and following an honorable discharge, he attended graduate school at Fisk University in Nashville, Tennessee, where he also taught biology, botany, and parasitology.

He graduated from Meharry Medical College in Nashville, Tennessee in 1963 and interned at Homer G. Phillips Hospital in St. Louis, Missouri, and completed a residency and fellowship in surgery at Freedmen's Hospital at Howard University in Washington, DC in 1968.

He practiced general and vascular surgery in Washington for thirty years and retired in 2003 to work full time with the Washington, DC, Department of Health as medical director.

In October 2001, following the anthrax event in DC, he helped provide prophylactic antibiotics to over 30,000 DC residents.

He received a master's degree as a *Scholar Studiorum Superiorum* in Bio-Hazardous Threat Agents and Emerging

Infectious Diseases from Georgetown University in DC in 2007.

He is currently an emeritus clinical associate professor of surgery at Howard University and an emeritus fellow of the American College of Nutrition.

He has been married to Shirley Jones from Charleston, West Virginia for fifty-four years, and they had four children: Thomas Junior, Christine, Kathryne, and Maria, who is deceased.

Printed in the United States
by Baker & Taylor Publisher Services